Cambridge Elements

Elements in Historical Theory and Practice
edited by
Daniel Woolf
Queen's University, Ontario

TESTIMONY AND HISTORICAL KNOWLEDGE

Authority, Evidence and Ethics in Historiography

Jonas Ahlskog
Åbo Akademi University, Finland

Shaftesbury Road, Cambridge CB2 8EA, United Kingdom

One Liberty Plaza, 20th Floor, New York, NY 10006, USA

477 Williamstown Road, Port Melbourne, VIC 3207, Australia

314–321, 3rd Floor, Plot 3, Splendor Forum, Jasola District Centre,
New Delhi – 110025, India

103 Penang Road, #05–06/07, Visioncrest Commercial, Singapore 238467

Cambridge University Press is part of Cambridge University Press & Assessment,
a department of the University of Cambridge.

We share the University's mission to contribute to society through the pursuit of
education, learning and research at the highest international levels of excellence.

www.cambridge.org
Information on this title: www.cambridge.org/9781009709392
DOI: 10.1017/9781009447041

© Jonas Ahlskog 2025

This publication is in copyright. Subject to statutory exception and to the provisions of relevant collective licensing agreements, with the exception of the Creative Commons version the link for which is provided below, no reproduction of any part may take place without the written permission of Cambridge University Press & Assessment.

An online version of this work is published at doi.org/10.1017/9781009447041 under a Creative Commons Open Access license CC-BY 4.0

When citing this work, please include a reference to the DOI 10.1017/9781009447041

First published 2025

A catalogue record for this publication is available from the British Library

ISBN 978-1-009-70939-2 Hardback
ISBN 978-1-009-44702-7 Paperback
ISSN 2634-8616 (online)
ISSN 2634-8608 (print)

Cambridge University Press & Assessment has no responsibility for the persistence or accuracy of URLs for external or third-party internet websites referred to in this publication and does not guarantee that any content on such websites is, or will remain, accurate or appropriate.

For EU product safety concerns, contact us at Calle de José Abascal, 56, 1°, 28003 Madrid, Spain, or email eugpsr@cambridge.org

Testimony and Historical Knowledge

Authority, Evidence and Ethics in Historiography

Elements in Historical Theory and Practice

DOI: 10.1017/9781009447041
First published online: August 2025

Jonas Ahlskog
Åbo Akademi University, Finland
Author for correspondence: Jonas Ahlskog, jonahlsk@abo.fi

Abstract: This Element explores the relation between historiography and testimony as a question about what it means to know and understand the past historically. In contrast with the recent rapprochement between memory accounts and history in historical theory, the Element argues for the importance of attending to conceptually distinct relations to past actions and events in historical thinking compared with testimony. The conceptual distinctiveness of history is elucidated by placing historical theory in dialogue with the epistemology of testimony and classical philosophy of history. By clarifying the rejection of testimony inherent in the evidential paradigm of modern historical research, this Element provides a thoroughgoing account of the ways in which historical knowledge and understanding relates to testimony. The argument is that the role of testimony in historiography is fundamentally shaped by the questioning-activity at the core of critical historical research. This title is also available as Open Access on Cambridge Core.

Keywords: Historical theory, Philosophy of History, Historical knowledge, Testimony, Historiography

© Jonas Ahlskog 2025

ISBNs: 9781009709392 (HB), 9781009447027 (PB), 9781009447041 (OC)
ISSNs: 2634-8616 (online), 2634-8608 (print)

Contents

1 Introduction   1
2 From Authority to Evidence   3
3 Testimony and Facts   18
4 Testimony, Understanding and Ethics   33
5 Conclusion   57

   Bibliography   60

1 Introduction

First-person accounts of past actions and events by historical agents – typically in the form of diaries, letters, autobiographies and reports – provide an essential and unique source of information for historical research. Considering that such testimonial material is ubiquitously used in historiography, a central question for the philosophy and theory of history is: What kind of epistemic, hermeneutic and ethical relations are there between testimony and history as a form of knowledge and thought? This foundational question has been discussed by seminal historians and philosophers of history from antiquity to the present. Currently, however, there is undoubtedly a revitalized interest in the role of testimony in historical research. This interest stems, on the one hand, from the general turn towards experience and memory, and, on the other, from the demise of narrativism in favour of philosophies of history that highlight the historian's multiple relations to the past.[1] In both historical theory and practice, the rise of testimony connects intimately with concerns for researching disadvantaged persons and communities that may be available only by way of memory accounts.

This Element reengages fundamental questions about what it means to think historically about the past and how this relates to testimony. The Element aims to offer, (i) a deeper understanding of the ways in which testimony has a valid role to play in historical research, and (ii) conceptual clarification for defending the distinctiveness and value of critical historical research in relation to testimony. Much contemporary work in the field tends to downplay the difference between history and memory accounts, sometimes even blurring the distinction between them completely.[2] This Element, on the contrary, argues for the importance of articulating conceptual and methodological distinctions between testimony and historical thinking. It is only by way of clear conceptual distinctions that one can correctly appreciate the role of testimony in historical research, as well as the nature of the historian's ethical responsibility as a critic of memory.

The thematic core of this element is the tension between testimony and the evidential paradigm of modern historical research.[3] According to this paradigm, modern historical research proceeds by way of the historical-critical method, and this method relates to all past material as evidence from which historians infer answers to their own questions. At the centre of this paradigm is the supposition that modern historical knowledge is inherently conjectural: historians observe certain traces from the past; they pose a hypothesis about what

---

[1] Day, "Relations with the Past"; Paul, *Key Issues*; Ohara, *Philosophy of History*.
[2] Stone, "History, Memory, Testimony." [3] Ginzburg, "Clues."

caused them; the traces serve as evidence to confirm or falsify their hypotheses. This most basic and constitutive idea of modern historical research has been elaborated on by many seminal philosophers of history. One of the most sophisticated, and certainly most influential, articulations of the evidential paradigm was delivered in R. G. Collingwood's classic work, *The Idea of History* (1946 [1993]). His account will serve as a central point of reference for explicating the distinctiveness of historical thinking in this Element. Naturally, the classical account of the evidential paradigm by Collingwood and other formative authors will be placed in dialogue with present concerns and developments in the philosophy and theory of history.

The evidential paradigm is confronted with two significant challenges from contemporary developments in research on testimony. The first challenge concerns questions about knowledge of facts in history and comes primarily from the thriving field of epistemology of testimony in analytic philosophy. This is a question about to what extent there is room for testimonial knowledge within the evidential paradigm of history. The second challenge, which is more discussed in historical theory, concerns questions about historical understanding and comes from the general turn towards memory and experience within the humanities. This is a question about to what extent historical understanding is conceptually distinct from understanding the past via testimony. The motive for assessing these challenges is not to reestablish outdated claims to objectivity for historical research, but to develop the idea of history as a critical form of thought that is found in classical accounts. Concurrently, this elaboration of classical accounts clarifies the ways in which critical historical research methods have an enduring and stable place within the discipline, despite the rise and fall of different theoretical trends and turns.[4]

This Element does not offer empirical research on historical writing in relation to social and judicial concerns related to testimony, which would be a book about the history and anthropology of historical research. Rather, I provide a philosophical elucidation of the ways in which historical thinking is methodologically and conceptually distinct from testimonial knowledge and understanding. Consequently, given the conceptual focus, there are three important research fields concerning testimony and history that fall outside the scope of this Element: (i) practical methodology for evaluating testimony, including witness psychology and probability calculus, (ii) history and the law and (iii) methods for the co-creation of source material in oral history.[5] Still, the results may indeed have implications for practitioners in the aforementioned

---

[4] Tosh, *Pursuit of History*.
[5] See, instead, Saupe and Roche, "Testimonies in Historiography"; Abrams, *Oral History Theory*; Wilson, *Writing History*; Tucker, *Historiographic Reasoning*; Jardine, "Explanatory Genealogies."

fields as well. My research focus will be on conceptual analysis for articulating the ways in which the basic presuppositions, a priori concepts and principles of modern historical research relate to knowledge and understanding by way of testimony.

The Element is thematically ordered but also seeks to do justice to the ways in which arguments and theories chronologically develop as responses to earlier positions. In the second section, I articulate the ways in which the limitation of testimonial reliance is inextricably linked with the Rankean paradigm of scientific and archive-based historical research. The autonomy of history from testimony was to become a key part of the self-image of the professional historian. In the third section, I analyze the claim for autonomy in relation to recent critiques that emphasize the historian's dependence on testimony for establishing basic facts about the past. Considering this critique, I argue that the claim for autonomy needs moderation and conceptual clarification considering different forms of testimonial reliance. For this task, historical theory is placed in dialogue with the epistemology of testimony. In the fourth section, the focus turns towards questions about historical understanding and recent arguments for subsuming historical thought under the conceptual umbrella of cultural memory. The (perceived) consequence is a rapprochement between historical understanding and the understanding of past events offered in witness accounts. In response, I argue that the conceptual distinctiveness of historical understanding can be defended by clarifying the ways in which history and memory accounts necessarily involve different logics of relating to the past, which is not to deny that individual historians always have multiple relations to the past. Finally, the arguments for autonomy will be put to work for articulating the historian's ethical responsibility in relation to testimony.

2 From Authority to Evidence

The concept of testimony has many different layers of meaning, and not all of them are relevant for this Element. Etymologically, the English word "testimony" derives from the Latin word *testis*, referring to a disinterested third-party witness. This root is often contrasted with the Latin word *superstes*, which refers to witnesses speaking about events from first-hand experience. Within this latter category, one may also distinguish between witnesses who suffered and perished, and witnesses who suffered and survived. The sense of *testis* is crucial for the juridical definition of testimony as a form of courtroom evidence, while the distinction between different kinds of suffering is fundamental for the religious meaning of testimony as martyrdom.[6] The most important sense of

---

[6] Van der Heiden, *Voice of Misery*, 193–194.

testimony for historiography, however, concerns not testimony as a distinct object or experience but rather as a certain kind of *epistemic relation* between historians and statements by historical agents. Concerning this relation, Collingwood provided a stipulative definition for the concept of testimony within historical research. Collingwood argued:

> When the historian accepts a ready-made answer to some question he has asked, given him by another person, this other person is called his 'authority', and the statement made by such an authority and accepted by the historian is called 'testimony.'[7]

The distinctive question about testimony in historiography concerns the transmission of knowledge, belief and understanding of past actions and events *between historical agents and the historian*. By and large, Collingwood's stipulative definition corresponds with the meaning of testimony in contemporary epistemology. Within the latter, testimony is an umbrella term for all those instances in which we form a belief, or acquire knowledge and understanding, based on what others have told us.[8] Such reliance on testimony is ubiquitous and exemplified whenever we, for instance, ask for road directions, read the newspaper or accept the word of a friend.

Testimony denotes an *epistemic source*. Unlike other sources – such as memory, inference, perception and introspection – testimony depends on the cognitive operations of another person (their observations, attentiveness, decisions about what to share, etc.). It follows from this definition that, for historiography, the principal question concerning testimony is not about whether a particular testimony falls under the label of *testis* or *superstes*, nor about whether the witness making a statement perished or survived. Such concerns are, of course, relevant within specific investigations. But the key question at issue is a normative and philosophical one about how history, as a specific form of knowledge and thought, can and should relate to all forms of testimony from historical agents about the past under investigation. Additionally, there is a question about testimony in relation to knowledge and belief transmission between contemporary historians. That question is not, however, specific to historiography but a subcategory of the general concern about trust within all scientific communities.[9]

There are two distinct ways in which testimony has been either limited or rejected as an epistemic source in modern historical research. The first way is the *historical-critical limitation* of testimonial reliance, epitomized in the

---

[7] Collingwood, *Idea of History*, 256.   [8] Gelfert, "Testimony."
[9] This general discussion is beyond the scope of this Element. For a classical account, see Hardwig, "Role of Trust."

Rankean paradigm of critical history, and the other is the *conceptual rejection* of testimony that belongs to the evidential paradigm. Before articulating that distinction, however, it is important to acknowledge that the use of testimony in history is as old as the discipline itself. Indeed, in the *Histories*, Herodotus of Halicarnassus (484–425 BC) relied centrally on accounts from eyewitnesses. Equally old is the historian's skepticism of eyewitnesses, as expressed in the work of Herodotus's contemporary, Thucydides (454–396 BC). In his introduction to *The Peloponnesian War*, Thucydides complained that "eye-witnesses did not report the same specific events in the same way, but according to individual partisanship or ability to remember."[10] Nevertheless, the principal method of premodern history was essentially about compiling accounts from reliable testimony, where "reliability" was often a function of the worldly and/or religious standing of the informant. The social and political role of the historian was to sing the songs of glorious rulers, venerated traditions and conquests of the past that had been transmitted to the historian via present or past eyewitness testimony. Testimonial reliance was the unquestioned bedrock of historical knowledge for premodern historiography – at least, this is the image offered by pioneers of Western, modern scientific history.[11] Most importantly for this Element, the limitation of testimonial reliance was a cornerstone of the historical-critical method – a mode of inquiry that became the global paradigm for professional historical research from the late nineteenth century onwards.[12]

2.1 The Limitation of Testimonial Reliance in Modern History

In modern historical research, the limitation of testimonial reliance is accelerated by the scientization of historiography with the advent of nineteenth-century historicism.[13] Naturally, this process is shaped by general views of science in the eighteenth and nineteenth centuries. Following Aristotle's lead, all major early modern philosophers excluded history from the realm of science – some even ranked history as the lowest grade of knowledge. The criteria of science proper, so to speak, were (logically) demonstrable knowledge by way of the necessary and universal operations of a syllogism, as Aristotle had thought. The subject matter of history, however, was the particular and the contingent, this or that person, matters of fact that could all, logically speaking, be otherwise. Even

---

[10] Thucydides, *Peloponnesian War*, 14.
[11] The history of history is, of course, much more complex. Cf. Woolf, *Concise History*.
[12] Woolf, *Concise History*, 8.
[13] Skepticism of testimony and oral tradition belongs, however, to the development of historical-critical methods which predate the rise of historicism. See, for example, Woolf, *Social Circulation of the Past*. In this Element, I use "historicism" only as a generic label for the reform of historiography that was led primarily by German idealists during the nineteenth century. The meaning of "historicism" is contested, for discussion see D'Amico, "Historicism."

worse, historians rarely had first-hand acquaintance with the particulars they wrote about but had to rely on the word of others. The word of others, in turn, was the helpless prey of Pyrrhonic skepticism concerning the reliability of all judgement and observation. In other words, history was about as far from science and certainty as one could get, just barely above mere opinion. Famous philosophers, such as Hobbes and Descartes, derided historical knowledge as the variable product of experience and authority, never reason.[14] The status of historical propositions as inherently unscientific was mirrored in the view that the historian was himself a kind of eyewitness to the past – a "man of affairs" whose reliability increased proportionally with his proximity to the events at issue.[15]

Against this background, history could become a science only by rejecting the supposition that historical knowledge was completely at the mercy of testimonial reliance. This is precisely what historicists did. As Frederick Beiser has argued, nineteenth-century historicists vindicated the scientific status of history by questioning the widespread thesis that historical propositions must be accepted on faith alone.[16] The fundamental claim was that history was indeed a science because it had its own method of acquiring knowledge and understanding about the past, and that this method did not itself rely on mere faith in testimony. The historian's method is perhaps best described as a critical logic of questions and answers concerning the reliability and meaning of all historical propositions. Such questions are, for example: What were the sources of a particular claim about the past? Are those sources reliable? What can one conjecture from comparing different testimonies? Most importantly, against Pyrrhonism, nineteenth-century historicists emphasized that modern historical research does not rely on testimonial sources alone. The modern historian may use relics from the past, such as coins, medals, inscriptions, and monuments and so on, as physical sources for criticizing testimony.[17] The very fact that the historian's questions can be raised, and sometimes answered, showed that historical propositions were indeed a form of knowledge. Consequently, by having a method of its own, history could claim the status of a science that produces not logically demonstrable truths but probable propositions about the past.[18]

The source criticism of the historical-critical method brought profound changes to the role of testimony in history. The methods themselves have their

---

[14] Beiser, "Historicism," 8.
[15] Woolf, *Concise History*, 24, 89; Eskildsen, "Relics of the Past," 71.
[16] Beiser, "Historicism," 8. As such, this idea is not a nineteenth century novelty. See, for example, Grafton, *Footnote*.
[17] Eskildsen, "Relics of the Past," 71–73. [18] Eskildsen, "Inventing the Archive," 11.

roots in biblical criticism, classical philology and comparative linguistics. It was from these disciplines that a critical methodology was imported and further developed in the nineteenth-century version of scientific historiography.[19] This critical methodology consisted chiefly of theories for the evaluation of the fidelity of the information chains that produced the historian's sources and a concomitant reevaluation of cognitive values: trust in the authority of testimony and tradition was replaced by critique and suspicion of the truth-value of material from the past. The most well-known example of this development is undoubtedly Leopold von Ranke's (1795–1886) school of critical history. Ranke's role in this process was not primarily that of an innovator – for the critical methodology that Ranke endorsed was mostly borrowed from others – but as the prime organizer of an influential paradigm for professional historical research. The most fundamental feature of this new Rankean paradigm was the idea that the historian's source material must be placed at the heart of historical study.

For Ranke's school, one form of source material was valued above all others: the archive document. As Kasper Risbjerg Eskildsen has argued, it was with Ranke that the archive became the main site for producing historical knowledge.[20] The historian must, according to the Rankean paradigm, study archive material based on rigorous source criticism and a clear distinction between primary and secondary sources. Among all the material that historians may use to support their accounts, the primary sources are of the highest value. Primary sources are documents either produced by or contemporary with the very events that the historian studies – either as descriptions or expressions – and will thereby allow the historian to study the past directly; without the subsequent distortions of traditional accounts of the events produced at a later date (secondary sources). As Georg Iggers has argued, Ranke's most famous and discussed dictum – to study the past *"wie es eigentlich gewesen"* (as it really happened) – states that the historian's task is to go beyond traditional accounts and refrain from moralizing judgements.[21] Thus, Ranke's seminal distinctions as well as his famous dictum *limit* the historian's dependence on testimony. This limitation comes in two different forms: (i) reliance on testimony from historical agents was relativized in relation to other testimony and non-testimonial source material, and (ii) the testimony of traditional accounts, essentially previous historians, was critiqued, or by-passed, with the focus on primary sources.

The Rankean revolution centres on the empirical concept of primary sources. This means that the key question is: What material from the past is the best kind

---

[19] Tucker, *Knowledge of the Past*, 46–91.   [20] Eskildsen, "Archival Turn."
[21] Iggers, "Historicism," 459.

of historical source material? Ranke himself favoured primary sources in the form of written archive documents, typically confidential diplomatic reports.[22] Staying true to his quest for authentic primary sources, it was only natural that Ranke himself was one of the chief instigators of expanding the amount of available historical source material by vast archive explorations in Prussia, Austria, Venice and the Papacy.[23] Still, the sources relevant for Ranke were circumscribed by his focus on the history of politics and the state, which meant that the primary sources were, accordingly, material relating to the political bodies under investigation. Subsequently, historians have expanded the range of source material to include all kinds of material remains from the past. This development starts on a more comprehensive scale already with Johan Huizinga's use of visual evidence, and, later, greatly influenced by the Annales School and Marc Bloch's arguments for inferring the past from our present landscape. The rise of "history from below" during the twentieth century – investigating the past from the perspective of class, gender and everyday life – has naturally meant that altogether new kinds of primary sources became relevant for historical research.

The starting point for Ranke's scientific history was *not* the historian's questions, concepts, ideas or hypotheses. On the contrary, objective research can only start by freeing oneself from such notions since they are, of course, shaped by the historian's own preconceptions. Scientific history begins, instead, with the very archive material upon which everyone can fix their attention, that is, the primary sources themselves.[24] For the Rankean historian, the value of the source material is tantamount to the authenticity and accuracy it shows itself to have by way of external and internal source criticism.[25] If only the historian freed himself from bias, the application of the historical-critical method would allow the primary sources to automatically reveal the past as it really happened. Past reality was not veiled for the Rankean historian but visible to the naked eye – were it not for the blindness caused by preconceptions and bias.[26] This attitude was epitomized in a famous quote in which Ranke exclaimed, "[I] wish that I could as it were dissolve myself and only let the things speak, the mighty powers appear."[27] Ranke did not, as Chris Lorenz puts it, acknowledge that all observation is theory-laden, which is common in present-day philosophy of science.[28]

Tellingly, the very word for "source" (*Quelle*), which gains currency within the German historicist tradition in the early nineteenth century, embodies the Rankean idea of accessing the past directly through primary sources. Suggesting images of

---

[22] Eskildsen, "Archival Turn," 442–443.
[23] Grafton, *Footnote*, 50–53.
[24] Bentley, "Turn towards 'Science'," 20.
[25] Day, *Philosophy of History*, 20–21.
[26] Bentley, "Turn towards 'Science'," 19.
[27] Ranke quoted in Eskildsen, "Inventing the Archive," 19.
[28] Lorenz, "Scientific Historiography," 398.

pure water flowing from a well spring, the term betrays romantic notions of the historian's untainted access to past reality through authentic, primary source material. Thus, the metaphoric sense of "source" tends to obscure the fundamental distinction between the data conveyed by the sources and historical knowledge. In the grips of this confusion, Grafton argues, Ranke tended to view specific kinds of archive documents as "transparent windows to past states and events rather than colorful reconstructions of them, whose authors [...] often wished to convince their own audience of a personal theory rather than simply to tell what happened."[29] This confusion was not, of course, shared by all historicists at the time. As Johann Gustav Droysen (1808–1884) already argued, source material does not speak for itself but stands in need of the historian's analytical and interpretive skills to become historical knowledge.[30]

It is important to emphasize the restricted, empiricist extension of Ranke's methodological revolution in historiography.[31] The Rankean revolution limits but does *not* reject reliance on the testimony of historical agents from the domain of scientific history. What it does reject is the authority of traditional accounts, in favour of attending to primary sources, as well as the acceptance of statements by historical agents at face value without corroboration. Scientific history does not depend on faith in testimony alone. But this is not a movement against testimonial reliance as such. Instead, it is a movement in which the quest for the most authentic and reliable witnesses becomes the chief task of the scientific historian. Rankean historiography is, therefore, keenly interested in separating direct from indirect witness, as well as with evaluating the epistemic virtues that witnesses must possess to deserve the historian's belief.[32] As a matter of fact, the appeal to reliable eyewitnesses is crucial for Ranke's identification of primary sources with direct access to the past. As Ranke wrote:

> I can see the time approach when we no longer have to base modern history on reports, even those of contemporary historians – except to the extent that they had first–hand knowledge – to say nothing of derivative reworking of the sources. Rather we will construct it from the accounts of eye-witnesses and the most genuine and direct sources.[33]

In other words, although historians could not themselves observe the past first-hand, they could gaze into the past directly by way of the authentic archival documents and relics it left behind in the present.[34] Gazing into the past directly, however, was premised on the possibility of fulfilling the "founding myth" of

---

[29] Grafton, *Footnote*, 59–60. [30] Droysen, *Historik*.
[31] In other respects, Ranke was a typical German idealist, see Gil, "Leopold Ranke."
[32] Eskildsen, "Inventing the Archive." [33] Ranke quoted in Grafton, *Footnote*, 51.
[34] Eskildsen, "Relics of the Past," 81.

scientific historiography.[35] This was that describing the past objectively is indeed a real possibility for historians. As Lorenz has argued, this myth relies on three connected requirements which today seem completely unfulfillable.[36] First, historians must dissolve themselves at their desks, thereby allowing the primary sources to speak for themselves. Second, there must be a clean break between past and present, requiring perhaps 50–100 years of distance between historians and the object of their study. Without separating "historical time" from the present, historians cannot view the past objectively due to possible personal interest and involvement.[37] Third, the archival documents and relics themselves must be products of objective and impartial social processes. Ranke assumed that such processes were guaranteed by the state archive as a neutral repository of raw material from the past.

The conceptual product of the Rankean paradigm is the idea of a historical past that directly mirrors the past-as-actuality. This is an idea of a historical past for which the elimination of forgery, bias, partisanship, value judgements, preconceptions, and so on, automatically allows the truth of the past-as-actuality to be revealed in the historian's primary sources. On this conception, source criticism, as *Quellenforschung*, is *the* method of scientific history. The proper application of that method enables the historian, ideally, to see the past itself exposed 1:1 in its remains. If authenticated, testimony is one possible direct source to the past. As a result, this view of historical research narrows the historian's knowledge claims to information that withstands the trial of source criticism. It cares not for concerns about narration, interpretation or the silences of the archive, issues that were not to be fully engaged until the 1960s in mainstream historical theory. It was also this narrow conception of method that was canonized as scientific history in a series of manuals during the late nineteenth century, such as Ernst Bernheim's *Lehrbuch* (1889) and Charles-Victor Langlois and Charles Seignobos *Introduction* (1897). Both provide detailed explorations of best practices for allowing the past to arise as it originally was from the historian's authenticated source material.

2.2 The Conceptual Rejection of Testimony in Modern History

One finds a philosophically far more penetrating argument against testimonial reliance in Collingwood's work. This is not to say that Collingwood is unique, even if he undoubtedly was a great innovator in the philosophy of history. Collingwood was influenced by other philosophers of history, such as Giambattista Vico and Benedetto Croce, and ideas similar to Collingwood's

---

[35] Lorenz, "Scientific Historiography," 395.   [36] Lorenz, "Scientific Historiography," 394.
[37] Cf. Mudrovcic, *History of the Present Time*.

have been presented by hermeneuticians such as Wilhelm Dilthey, Heinrich Rickert and Hans-Georg Gadamer. But the main reason Collingwood deserves space paralleling the Rankean paradigm is his unrivalled influence in English-speaking philosophy and theory of history. This influence stretches far beyond the confines of academia – *The Idea of History* has been included on the *Times Literary Supplement*'s list of the most influential post-Second World War books.[38] Importantly, in contrast to most classical authors on the historical-critical method, Collingwood engaged the question of testimony in detail.[39] The reason for this is that Collingwood's very idea of history was developed in opposition to testimonial reliance. He argued that this opposition was a key characteristic of modern historical research. As we shall see, Collingwood's rejection of testimony relies on conceptual rather than empirical grounds.

Collingwood was not impressed by the philosophical underpinning of the Rankean model of scientific historiography. For Collingwood, Langlois's and Seignobos's methodology manual was "about as useful to the modern reader as would be a discussion of physics in which no mention was made of relativity."[40] This stark judgement is motivated by the fact that Collingwood disagreed with the most basic presupposition of the Rankean model of scientific history. Contrary to Ranke and his followers, Collingwood did not think that historical research starts with the source material. He explicitly derided "modern anti-scientific epistemologists" for their idea that "when we have made our minds a perfect blank we shall 'apprehend the facts'."[41] Scientific history did not, Collingwood argued, start with the source material but with questions posed by the historian. Collingwood was very clear on this point. He wanted to show that the "questioning-activity" is the "dominant factor in history, as it is in all scientific work."[42] Collingwood thereby argued that the Rankean historian got the wrong end of the stick: "you can't collect your evidence before you start thinking: because thinking means asking questions ...nothing is evidence except in relation to some definite question."[43] His fundamental argument was based on the insight that question and evidence are correlative concepts. Evidence *is* that which allows you to answer the question you are asking. As Collingwood argued:

> Everything is evidence which the historian can use as evidence. But what can he so use? It must be something here and now perceptible to him: this written page, this spoken utterance, this building, this finger-print. And of all the

---

[38] Van der Dussen, "Historical Imagination."
[39] For the most important discussions, see Collingwood, *Idea of History*, 33, 202–204, 234–245, 256–282, 487–492, and Collingwood, *Principles of History*, 66–67, 72–73, 80–81, 241, 245.
[40] Collingwood, *Idea of History*, 143. [41] Collingwood, *Idea of History*, 274.
[42] Collingwood, *Idea of History*, 273. [43] Collingwood, *Idea of History*, 281.

things perceptible to him there is not one which he might not conceivably use as evidence on some question, if he came to it with the right question in mind. The enlargement of historical knowledge comes about mainly through finding how to use as evidence this or that kind of perceived fact which historians have hitherto thought useless to them.[44]

Collingwood's argument has far-reaching consequences for the historian's relation to material from the past. Contrary to the Rankean model for scientific history, Collingwood's discussion is not about what kind of material the historian should favour, nor about the correct critical apparatus for assessing the authenticity, credibility and accuracy of the source material. In fact, Collingwood dissolves the very idea of there being such a thing as the best material or practical method for studying the past to be established independently of the historian's questioning-activity. Fundamentally, Collingwood's argument shows that the historian's relation to past material cannot be sufficiently explored empirically. Rather, what is needed is a philosophical investigation of the ways in which the questioning-activity *conceptually* disposes historians in relation to the material that they study.

For understanding the paradigmatic role of the questioning-activity in modern historical research, Collingwood provided a canonical story of how historiography freed itself from testimonial reliance.[45] According to Collingwood, history evolved immensely in the nineteenth and early twentieth centuries – it had, in his rather grandiose terms, gone through a "Copernican revolution."[46] Collingwood pictured this as a process in which historical thought became autonomous as historians rejected the authority of testimony. By autonomy, Collingwood means: "the condition of being one's own authority, making statements or taking action on one's own initiative and not because those statements or actions are authorized or prescribed by anyone else."[47] In essence, prerevolutionary history consisted of believing authorities upon testimony. Postrevolutionary history, on the contrary, is based on autonomous reasoning from evidence. Even if the metaphor of a "Copernican revolution" is extravagant, it does rightly single out a decisive feature of the change in the idea of history that Collingwood wanted to describe. The centre of gravity in history had moved from the authority of witnesses of the past to the historian as a self-authorizing scientist who constructs accounts of the past based on evidence.

---

[44] Collingwood, *Idea of History*, 246–247.
[45] Collingwood's story is, however, best read as an articulation of his philosophical concept of history rather than as a factually accurate history of history. For the latter, see Woolf, *Concise History*.
[46] Collingwood, *Idea of History*, 236, 240.   [47] Collingwood, *Idea of History*, 274–275.

This epistemological revolution in history was styled by Collingwood as a three-phase development. First came "scissors-and-paste" history, which was prerevolutionary, and after the revolution came "critical history" and finally "scientific history," or history proper, which is based on Collingwood's seminal notion of reenactment.[48] By scissors-and-paste history, Collingwood denotes a form of writing about the past that he dates to antiquity and the Middle Ages. Such writing about the past, considered pseudo-history by Collingwood, is conducted by excerpting and combining the testimonies of different authorities. By critical history Collingwood denotes a practice that he dates to the seventeenth century, in which historians engage in a systematic critique of the authorities to be included in their own narrative. Both scissors-and-paste and critical history, however, focus only on questions about the truth and falsity of statements by historical agents. In contrast, scientific history, or history proper, focuses on the meaning of past statements in relation to the historian's questioning-activity.

At the core of Collingwood's reasoning was a sharp conceptual distinction between testimony and evidence. Belief in testimony, Collingwood claimed, "stops ... where history begins."[49] In history proper, one does not merely believe the testimony of authorities. Rather, these "authorities" become only evidence from which historians, upon their own authority, infer answers to their own questions about the past. Collingwood goes so far as to say that not only is history independent of testimony; it has "no relation to testimony at all."[50] History is a wholly reasoned form of knowledge proceeding through questions, evidence and criticism. The criterion, therefore, of what is to be accepted as a historical fact is not the trustworthiness of a witness, but the historian's imaginative reconstruction and reenactment based on evidence. According to Collingwood, scientific history is practiced when the historian is "twisting a passage [by a historical agent] ostensibly about something different into an answer to the question he has decided to ask."[51]

For Collingwood, the epistemological foundation of history cannot be the authenticity of witness rapports. The autonomy of history, derived from the primacy of questions and imaginative reconstruction, implies that there is "nothing other than historical thought itself, by appeal to which its conclusion may be verified."[52] This argument entails that the criterion for what counts as a historical fact is not the trustworthiness of historical witnesses, but the historian's imaginative reconstruction and critical assessment of past actions and events based on a wide range of sources used as evidence. Given the

---

[48] Collingwood, *Idea of History*, 282–304, 257–266.   [49] Collingwood, *Idea of History*, 308.
[50] Collingwood, *Idea of History*, 203.   [51] Collingwood, *Idea of History*, 270.
[52] Collingwood, *Idea of History*, 243.

primacy of questions and imaginative reconstruction, it will ultimately be the historian, in critical dialogue with their community of peers, who determines which account of past actions and events that is most supported by the evidence and therefore to be labelled historical fact.

On Collingwood's view, historical fact is a dialogical concept in which the significance of actions and events of the past is seen in relation to the understanding and knowledge we have in our present historical context. If the historian simply received information about the past through testimony, in the manner of receiving a letter in the mail, then this information does not in itself constitute historical knowledge. History is not just a method for transferring information from the past to the present. If that were the case, historical knowledge would always be second rate to being contemporaneous with the past events themselves. The perfect experts on the causes of the Thirty Years' War would be people who lived at that time, while historians are at the mercy of the crumbs of information that they happened to leave behind. Naturally, this presupposes that people in the past already possessed the knowledge that historians pursue, which is precisely what Collingwood denies.[53]

On this score, there are similarities with Hans-Georg Gadamer's notion of a "fusion of horizons," and Gadamer was indeed explicit about his debts to Collingwood.[54] Historical knowledge and understanding do not proceed by somehow comparing (past) statements with the reality that they are about. Rather, it proceeds on the logic of question and answer – only by first understanding the question to which a statement was meant to be the answer can we understand that statement itself. As Gadamer points out, however, in this process it is always necessary to go beyond mere reconstruction. The meaning of a past statement is, in history, dependent not merely on the question it was meant to answer in the past but also on the question it is used to answer for the historian. In this process, historians necessarily bring in their own preunderstanding and cannot "avoid to think of what the author accepted unquestioningly."[55] This means that testimony can never be sufficient for acquiring what is properly called historical knowledge. What goes by that name is necessarily dependent on the historian's own horizon of understanding.

In sum, modern, scientific historians study past events that are not available to observation. The method of their study is to infer accounts of past events from something that is accessible to observation; namely, material traces in the present – the historian's evidence. Consequently, knowledge of the past is

---

[53] Cf. Collingwood, *Idea of History*, 447.
[54] Gadamer, *Truth and Method*, 363–364. There are also many important differences between Gadamer and Collingwood, see my *Primacy of Method*, 99–115.
[55] Gadamer, *Truth and Method*, 367.

properly called "historical" only to the extent that this knowledge is based on what the evidence at our disposal obliges us to believe about events in the past. Even if one may have arrived at the very same propositions about past actions and events by other means – say memory accounts, time travel or hearsay – then this would not qualify as historical knowledge. The reason being that knowledge does not count as historical simply for being about this or that event or action in the past, but only if the knowledge in question has been produced by way of the historical method of inferring claims about the past from evidence in the present. Thus, the data about the past that testimony may carry are, by definition, not historical knowledge of the past.

2.3 The Historical Past of Method

The conceptual rejection of testimony has – often without apparent influence from Collingwood – been endorsed by many seminal authors in historical theory.[56] The historian Carlo Ginzburg labelled it the arrival of an "evidential paradigm" in historical research.[57] In this context, the concept of paradigm is not used in the Kuhnian sense of methodological agreement and uniformity. Rather, when Ginzburg speaks of an "evidential paradigm" he refers to a large-scale transformation of the historian's basic understanding of their source material. According to Ginzburg, modern historical knowledge is conjectural by nature: historians observe certain traces; they pose a hypothesis about what caused them; the traces serve as evidence to confirm or falsify their hypotheses. All source material of the past – from the farmer's pots and ploughs to the philosopher's treatises and testimony from both worldly and religious leaders – should be treated *not* as authorities to be believed based on the pedigree of their origin but merely as evidence.[58]

The key feature of the evidential paradigm is *not* the idea of understanding source material as relics or remains. This was already acknowledged by nineteenth century advocates of scientific history such as Ranke and Bernheim. The idea of remains is, as such, fully compatible with the ambition to gaze at the past directly. What distinguishes the evidential paradigm is, instead, a distinct epistemic relation to the object of investigation – it stipulates that *all* kinds of source material should be subsumed under the category of evidence. If the source material is understood as evidence, the relevance of that material is dependent on the specific questioning–activity of the historian. As Collingwood

---

[56] For example, Bloch, *Historian's Craft*; Foucault, "Nietzsche, Genealogy, History"; Ricoeur, *Memory, History, Forgetting*.
[57] Ginzburg, "Clues."
[58] I have criticised the one-dimensional evidentialism of Ginzburg's ideas in my book *Primacy of Method*, 132–152.

showed, evidence is never relevant in and of itself. Rather, it is relevant only in its capacity for answering the question that the historian has decided to ask. In other words, there is an internal connection between the evidential use of source material and the autonomy of history as a discipline.

It is difficult to overestimate the significance of the evidential paradigm for the idea of modern historical research. It is by treating sources as evidence that history qualifies in the general category of science. Contrary to poetry and prose fiction, historical accounts of the past must be constrained, on the one hand by the available source material, and on the other, by the ability of historians to prove the reliability and validity of their inferences from sources used as evidence to a community of peers. Tellingly, Marc Bloch endorsed the arrival of the evidential paradigm as "a glorious victory of mind over its material."[59] This paradigmatic change came to reshape the historian's self-image as one in which a radical break had occurred in contrast with their premodern colleagues.

The evidential paradigm freed historians from epistemological subordination. As Bloch wrote, the memoirs of Saint-Simon[60] may frequently give us nothing but fictitious news about the events of the reign of Louis XIV, but they cannot, when used as evidence in spite of themselves, fail to express the mentality of a great noble at the court of the Sun King. By treating the material from the past as evidence, historians could know "far more of the past than the past itself thought good to tell."[61] Inspired by the glorious victory, it was not uncommon that testimony was disqualified as an altogether unreliable epistemic source among proponents of the evidential paradigm.[62] As Bloch argued, for the historian, there is no such thing as a "good eyewitness"; all witness accounts are limited in their perspective, subjective, and dependent on the variant faculty of memory.[63]

A distinct idea of the historical past is born with the evidential paradigm. As I argued, the paradigmatic Rankean view of the historical past is one in which the historian apprehends the past directly by objectively gazing its authentic remains – if historians have been able to make their minds a perfect blank. In contrast, the historical past of the evidential paradigm is the outcome of the historian's questioning-activity. While the Rankean historian observes the past directly in the sources, the historical past for the evidential paradigm is a product of method.[64] The latter is not an entity that the historian somehow

---

[59] Bloch, *Historian's Craft*, 53.   [60] Louis de Rouvroy, duc de Saint-Simon (1675–1755).
[61] Bloch, *Historian's Craft*, 53.
[62] For discussion, see Saupe and Roche, "Testimonies in Historiography," 67–71.
[63] Bloch, "Reflections," 1.
[64] It is beyond the scope of this Element to engage debates about the reality of the historical past. For discussion, see my *Primacy of Method*, 1–18, 45–78.

observes in the remains, but a past constructed to explain the evidence in relation to the question historians have decided to ask. This very attitude to material from the past was by Collingwood defined as historical thinking:

> [H]istorical thinking means nothing else than interpreting all the available evidence with maximum degree of skill. It does not mean discovering what really happened, if what 'really happened' is anything other than 'what the evidence indicates.'[65]

Consequently, the questioning-activity of the historian introduces a break between the past-as-actuality and the past as constructed from evidence in historical research.[66] The latter is, as Michael Oakeshott argued, a past that can only be found in history books.[67] For the Rankean historian, this would be a major drawback. The goal of scientific history was to know the past-as-actuality, revealed in the most authentic primary sources, freed from the historian's preconceptions. Refuting this aim is a fundamental part of the conceptual rejection of testimony in the philosophy of history. The truth historians are looking for, Collingwood wrote, was not "possessed, ready-made, by the writer whom we are studying."[68] Similarly, Arthur Danto argued "the whole point of history is *not* to know about actions as witnesses might, but as historians do, in connection with later events and as part of temporal wholes."[69] In other words, testimony is rejected because historiography involves a distinct form of understanding that goes beyond the knowledge and understanding of events that historical witnesses could possibly have had.

Seminal historians and historical theorists were certainly very keen on separating historical knowledge from testimony. Less certain is whether this separation amounts to a coherent position. Would a wholesale rejection of testimony not also undermine the historian's task of establishing basic factual claims about "what happened" in the past? For example, to what extent was the Winter Palace plundered when it was seized by the Bolsheviks on 26 October 1917? Eyewitness accounts of those present at the time would be vital sources of information for every attempt to establish what happened at a factual level. That knowledge may, in turn, serve as material for historical research concerning, say, moral norms and discipline during the Russian Revolution. Consequently, how would the historian's account of the past ever get off the ground if *all* testimony is rejected as not only unreliable but also irrelevant for a distinctly historical way of knowing the past? In the following section, I will address this fundamental objection and clarify the conceptual

---

[65] Collingwood, "Limits of Historical Knowledge," 99.
[66] Cf. Goldstein, *Philosophical Essays*. [67] Oakeshott, *On History*, 33.
[68] Collingwood, *Idea of History*, 377. [69] Danto, *Analytical Philosophy of History*, 183.

rejection of testimony for establishing historical facts. Thereafter, in the fourth section, I proceed to the relation between testimony and historical understanding.

3 Testimony and Facts

It is today commonplace to argue that advocates of the evidential paradigm, especially Collingwood, overstated their case against testimony.[70] The overstatement was not about whether testimony is a useful source of historical evidence. Instead, the claim is that advocates of the evidential paradigm overstated the historian's epistemic autonomy. By doing so they denied the role of testimony as a form of knowledge about the past in historical research. In response, it is argued that the historian is as dependent on testimony as we are for establishing everyday facts in the present. This contention challenges the core claim of the evidential paradigm; namely, that history is an autonomous form of knowledge and, therefore, independent from reliance on testimony.

The argument against the autonomy of history has two distinct dimensions. First, there is the *ontological* argument that historical source material, as well as the archive institution itself, is fundamentally constituted by testimony to an extent that classical authors failed to acknowledge. Ultimately, the historian's access to the past is possible only by way of source material that, in one way or another, is dependent on human testimony. Thus, the key question cannot be about rejecting testimony, which would be impossible, but about historicizing its production and preservation. Second, there is the *epistemological* argument that classical authors were simply too skeptical about the role of testimony as a source of epistemic justification in relation to historical facts. This skepticism, it is argued, was caused by Enlightenment ideals of epistemological individualism that gravely underestimate our dependence on the word of others in all knowledge and belief acquisition.[71] When those ideals are rejected, one should recognize testimony as an independent source of epistemic justification for historiography, just like in everyday knowledge and belief acquisition. In the following, I assess the strengths and weaknesses of the conceptual rejection of testimony in relation to historical facts.

3.1 Material Dependence

One of the most influential recent proponents of the ontological argument is Paul Ricoeur. In his last major work, *Memory, History and Forgetting*, Ricoeur

---

[70] Coady, *Testimony*; Day; *Philosophy of History*; Tozzi, "Role of Testimony"; Tucker, *Knowledge of the Past*; Ricoeur, *Memory, History, Forgetting*; Saupe and Roche, "Testimonies in Historiography."

[71] Coady, *Testimony*. For the relation to conceptions of written language and orality, see Hudson, *Writing and European Thought*.

develops a position that seems to go directly against the basic claims of the evidential paradigm. According to Ricoeur, testimony constitutes the very bedrock of historiography – as the "womb of history."[72] He contends that the practice of historical research would be unimaginable without testimony. Ricoeur's argument is framed in opposition to the archival turn of modern historiography. He writes:

> [W]e must not forget that everything starts, not from the archives, but from testimony, and that, whatever may be our lack of confidence in principle in such testimony, we have nothing better than testimony, in the final analysis, to assure ourselves that something did happen in the past, which someone attests having witnessed in person, and that the principal, and at times our only, recourse, when we lack other types of documentation, remains the confrontation among testimonies.[73]

This passage highlights several important features of the ontological case for testimony. First, it is certainly true that, given the lack of other kinds of documentation, eyewitness testimony must have a fundamental role for the historian's account of past events. As Ricoeur rightly emphasizes, how would knowledge in such cases be possible at all without relying on the attestation of those present at the events themselves?[74] Second, Ricoeur is very much to the point when he claims that historiography does *not* start in the archive. As he writes with reference to Michel de Certeau's work, the archive is "not just a physical or spatial place, it is also a social one."[75] In contrast to what Ranke and his followers assumed, the archive is not a neutral site of knowledge production that would somehow have the power of "assuring the objectivity of historical knowledge."[76] Rather, the archive material is always already a product of power relations that determine what is considered worth preserving.[77]

Historiography is not only materially dependent on the testimony of historical agents, but also on the decisions of archivists for the very existence of the material itself. Not only is the archive selective on a social and political basis, but the very idea of a complete archive is also incoherent. "[A]rchive as much as you like: something will always be left out,"[78] as Pierre Nora exclaimed. In other words, the historian's source material seems to depend on other human beings all the way down.

Ricoeur's argument about the necessary social relations of source material offers a well-needed remedy for the fetishization of the archive in scientific

---

[72] Ricoeur, *Memory, History, Forgetting*, 87, 95.
[73] Ricoeur, *Memory, History, Forgetting*, 147. [74] Cf. Ginzburg, "Just One Witness."
[75] Ricoeur, *Memory, History, Forgetting*, 167. [76] Ricoeur, *Memory, History, Forgetting*, 169.
[77] Foucault, *Archaeology of Knowledge*, 142–148.
[78] Quoted by Ricoeur, *Memory, History, Forgetting*, 169.

history. Nevertheless, the argument is of limited relevance for appreciating the specific role of testimony in relation to historical facts.

Ricoeur clearly relies on reasoning from what W.H. Dray called "vacuous contrasts."[79] To claim that source material in general is always, in one way or another, the product of either human observation or human relations is a truism. It is equally true and unproblematic to say that historical research is always only based on a selection of source material. But as Dray pointed out in relation to the latter, this does not yet say anything specific about history. The contrast is vacuous – if it is meant to somehow set history apart from other sciences – since the feature one has identified is shared by all the sciences. Consequently, one ends up with the platitude that historical knowledge, like knowledge in general, is dependent on human observations and relations. This line of reasoning will also inflate the concept of testimony colossally by including all material dependent on human beings, that is, everything from train tickets to assertions of an eyewitness. Obviously, this broad concept cannot do justice to the central historical research practice of comparing the assertions of a witness (testimony) not only with other testimonies but also with non-intentional material produced by the events under investigation. The ontological argument reveals the basic, material dependence on testimony in history, but it does not get us very far.

Ricoeur's womb-metaphor highlights our fundamental dependence on other human beings for information about the historical past. In general, we tend to underestimate the fact that "our observation" comes mostly from the observation of others, and this is all the truer for historians who may observe the evidence but never the past itself. Historiography does share this typically unrecognized and widespread dependence on the word of others. As Avishai Margalit writes "This [dependence] is true for all our walks of life: science, religion, history, court, and of course for our collective memory. . . . I am caught in a network of witnesses."[80] Important as these points are, this fundamental dependence was not denied by classical proponents of the evidential paradigm. For example, both Collingwood and Bloch readily acknowledged this basic form of reliance.[81] As Bloch famously wrote:

> "We are told that the historian is, by definition, absolutely incapable of observing the facts which he examines. No Egyptologist has ever seen Ramses. No expert on the Napoleonic Wars has ever heard the sound of the cannon of Austerlitz. We can speak of earlier ages only through the accounts of eye-witnesses."[82]

---

[79] Dray, *Philosophy of History*, 29. [80] Margalit, *Ethics of Memory*, 180–181.
[81] For this acknowledgement by Collingwood, see my *Primacy of Method*, 160–161.
[82] Bloch, *Historian's Craft*, 40.

Bloch continues by emphasizing that "[a] good half of all we see, is seen through the eyes of others," and that "all knowledge of mankind, to whatever time it applies, will always derive a large part of its evidence from others. In this respect, the student of the present is scarcely any better off than the historian of the past."[83] For Bloch, however, it is important to qualify this dependence by pointing out the relativizing input from material evidence. The "tracks" and "residues" of the past are things that the historian can indeed "see with his own eyes."[84]

It should now be clear that the challenge of testimony requires further specification. The key issue is not whether history *does* depend on information gained from relying on statements by other human beings. As we have seen, advocates of the evidential paradigm were not denying this basic dependence. The question at issue is, instead, what *kind* of dependence the historian's testimonial reliance amounts to. What does reliance on testimony mean in historical research? For this one must turn from the ontological domain towards questions about the epistemic relation between testimony and historical knowledge. In recent work, this epistemic relation has been articulated in efforts to align historical knowledge with the flourishing field of the epistemology of testimony in analytic philosophy.[85] The basic argument is that historiography is akin to knowing by testimony since historians too must rely on the word of others as epistemic justification.

3.2 Epistemic Dependence

It is impossible to assess the epistemic relevance of testimony for historiography without first defining the relevant meaning of testimony. While the ontological argument tends to broaden the concept of testimony, in (analytic) epistemology discussions testimony often denotes the specific speech acts of telling and/or asserting.[86] From such speech acts, it is argued, one may acquire *testimonial knowledge*. Given this focus on the nature of specific speech acts, testimony becomes a philosophical term of art for knowledge and belief acquisition via tellings. How to understand testimonial knowledge is, however, at the very heart of the debate. Roughly, the general idea is that we have testimonial knowledge when we believe something because someone tells us. The focus of the philosophical debate has been about the justification of testimonial knowledge, that is, whether it is acceptable to call testimony knowledge, and if so under what conditions.

There are two traditional camps in the epistemology of testimony: (i) reductionism or evidentialism, and (ii) non-reductionism or, later, "the assurance view." David Hume (1711–1776) is often construed as the father of

---

[83] Bloch, *Historian's Craft*, 41–42.   [84] Bloch, *Historian's Craft*, 45.
[85] Coady, *Testimony*; Tozzi, "Role of Testimony"; Day, *Philosophy of History*; Ahlskog, "Crisis of Testimony."
[86] For an overview, see Leonard, "Problems of Testimony."

reductionism, while Thomas Reid (1710–1796) is styled as the progenitor of non-reductionism. Reductionism has historically been dominant and is often considered the traditional position, but today there is a plethora of reductionist, non-reductionist and intermediate accounts.[87] The bone of contention between reductionists and non-reductionists is the source and character of epistemic justification. In brief, non-reductionists claim that testimony is a *sui generis* source of justification of knowledge, and reductionists claim that testimony can amount to knowledge only if supported by independent reasons for belief provided by the individual's own perception, memory and reasoning. However, the dispute is not about whether it is, in general, possible to transmit knowledge and belief via testimony. Both sides accept the commonsense fact that we do constantly learn about the world from what other people tell us. Rather, what reductionists deny, and non-reductionists confirm, is that beliefs based on testimony can be epistemically justified merely in virtue of the fact that another person has asserted the claim in question.

The most interesting question for historiography is the possibility of non-reductive testimonial knowledge. As we have seen, the role of reductive testimonial knowledge is, of course, commonplace in the ubiquitous practice of using testimony as historical evidence. In fact, this reductive practice is exemplified every time a historian compares the assertions of a witness with non-intentional evidence material. The case for non-reductive testimonial knowledge in historiography, however, was pioneered by C. A. J. Coady in his landmark book, *Testimony: A Philosophical Study* (1992). Coady's seminal book, which shaped subsequent discussions in the epistemology of testimony, argued that – contrary to the argument for autonomy by Collingwood and others – historiography is inherently dependent on non-reductive testimonial knowledge. Coady does not, however, discuss the ways in which historiography includes narration and analytical concepts, such as the Unification of Germany or the Renaissance. His claim is not that such notional totalities, beyond the perception of individuals, can be known by way of testimony. Coady is interested only in what he calls historical facts. Specifically, he is interested in facts that can be expressed in singular existential propositions, such as "In September 1830, there were three days of street-fighting in Brussels."[88] In other words, Coady emphasizes that there are indeed cases of facts about the past, contrary to Collingwood's claim, for which the truth of the matter was possessed ready-made by the historical agents themselves. As Coady argues,

---

[87] Leonard, "Problems of Testimony"; Kennedy, *History of Reasonableness*.
[88] Coady, *Testimony*, 234.

[S]ince the historian is seeking truths about the human past, his facts will be provided for him by those who lived in the past.... After all, if they do not provide it for him how else will he discover it? He cannot participate in or observe the events since they are, by definition, no longer accessible to such involvement. Consequently, the recorded testimony of the times would appear to be essential historical data, the very stuff of history.[89]

As a well-known proponent of non-reductionism, Coady's motive for discussing historiography was to show the soundness of that position in relation to historical facts. Coady's main philosophical argument is that the possibility of linguistic communication already guarantees some positive correlations between statements and facts. Understanding a language in use requires that one relates to some of the reports expressed in it as true. For how else would the hearers ever be able to assign content to the speaker's assertions – if they cannot presuppose that there is any reliable correlation between the speaker's assertions and the truth? The reductionist thesis is therefore found to be inherently flawed. Rejecting *all* testimony as inherently unreliable is not a coherent position. One cannot "understand what testimony is independently of knowing that it is, in any degree, a reliable form of evidence about the way the world is."[90] For Coady, epistemic reliance on testimony in historiography, as well as in everyday conversations, simply means that one must (logically) presuppose that the word of others is a reliable, but defeasible, source of information or data.

The main strength of Coady's argument is that it articulates features of testimonial reliance that historiography shares with everyday knowledge and belief transmission. The (a priori) reliability of testimony, as a logical presupposition of linguistic communication, holds, of course, for historiography in just the same way as it does in everyday situations. Thus, Coady's argument exposes the fallacy of rejecting *all* testimony as inherently unreliable. This argument, in turn, shows that the Enlightenment ideal of epistemological individualism is untenable also in historiography.[91] The very practice of comparing testimonies relies on giving credence to some testimony over others, which, ipso facto, prohibits the rejection of all testimonial reliance.

Contrary to what Coady believes, however, the fact that linguistic communication presupposes a norm of truthfulness does not warrant anti-reductionism about testimony.[92] The reason being, of course, that it is the very same norm that also makes untruthful testimony possible.[93] One cannot justify testimonial reliance in any individual case by pointing to the fact that global error is philosophically unthinkable.

---

[89] Coady, *Testimony*, 234.   [90] Coady, *Testimony*, 85.
[91] Coady, *Testimony*, 79–100, 233–249; Day, *Philosophy of History*, 44–49.
[92] Cf. Gelfert, *Critical Introduction*, 107–108.   [93] Cf. Kant, "On the Supposed Right."

In relation to historiography, the main weakness of Coady's argument is his failure to understand what philosophers of history, especially Collingwood, were rejecting in rejecting testimony from history. For Coady, the main aim was to show that testimony is a reliable form of evidence "about the way the world is."[94] From the start, he describes testimony as an attestation that "is evidence towards the settling of the matter."[95] In Coady's view, epistemic reliance upon testimony *is* a species of evidential inference in which the evidence happens to be the word of another person. No significant conceptual distinction can therefore be made between evidence and testimony for Coady. As I showed in the previous section, however, the rejection of testimony among classical philosophers of history is the result of stressing the very conceptual distinction that Coady neglects. The former argued that there is an important conceptual distinction between relating to source material as testimony *or* as evidence. Consequently, when classical philosophers of history rejected testimony, they were not, as Coady assumed, rejecting testimony as a species of evidence. On the contrary, they would all have agreed with Coady: in historical research, testimony is treated *as* evidence. Instead, what they rejected was testimony *as authority*.

As we saw, for Collingwood reliance upon testimony is specified as the distinctive act of believing another person on their say-so. This interpretation is strongly supported by the fact that Collingwood systematically connects the concept of testimony with relying on the authority of ready-made statements, and not with the mere act of using another person's statement as evidential input in one's own reasoning.[96] What one receives in testimony are assertions to be accepted simply upon the other person's authority. The main worry was that accepting a proposition on the mere say-so of another person seems – precisely as contemporary epistemologists argue – to involve a deferral of responsibility for the belief acquired from historians to the witnesses in the past.[97] If a historian simply accepted the say-so of an authority, Collingwood argued, then the latter would be responsible for what went into the historian's narrative.[98] That, in turn, is in conflict with the very job description of the modern historian who should be "relying on his own powers and constituting himself as his own authority."[99] Furthermore, as the next section shows, Collingwood's rejection was very much to the point since the social fact of

---

[94] Coady, *Testimony*, 85. [95] Coady, *Testimony*, 38.
[96] Collingwood, *Idea of History*, 17, 33, 260, 262, 264, 274, 278, 488; *Principles of History*, 66, 73, 245.
[97] Cf. McMyler, *Testimony*, 61–65. [98] Collingwood, *Idea of History*, 236–237, 256.
[99] Collingwood, *Idea of History*, 237.

deferral of responsibility, which non-reductive testimony involves, does not amount to epistemic justification.

3.3 Different Logics of Justification

As we have seen, the conceptual rejection of testimony from historiography should not be confused with rejecting the use of testimony as evidence. Classical philosophers of history did not reject testimony as evidence nor as a source of data, but rather testimony as a ready-made authoritative account of past events. Nevertheless, further specification of the distinctiveness of historical knowledge is needed. One may still ask: If it is sometimes legitimate to rely on testimony as ready-made, authoritative answers in everyday life, as it arguably is, then why are we not allowed to do so also in historical research? In other words, can testimony be something more than just evidence for the historian? These questions connect directly with ongoing discussions in the epistemology of testimony in which much attention has been given to questions about the categorical difference between relating to the word of others either as *evidence* or as *assurance*.[100] Richard Moran, one of the main advocates of this distinction, has argued that to accept a speaker's testimony is not to take it as good evidence for belief, but to believe what is said on their say-so, their assurance. When testimony is understood as assurance it is "the speaker who is believed, and belief in the proposition asserted follows from this."[101]

In Moran's work, assurance and evidence are distinct epistemic attitudes with different logics of justification. He explicates the difference with the following example: I look outside the window on a sunny day and see people bundled up in thick clothes. First, I consider their behaviour as evidence and draw the conclusion that it is colder outside than it otherwise looks. Second, my friend arrives and tells me that it is cold (or not). In the latter case, my friend's verbal behaviour is not *evidence* from which I make my own conclusions about the weather. My friend tells me something and I believe him. This means that my entitlement to believe is based not on my own assessment of what is said, but on the speaker's standing by his word. My friend gives me *assurance* that it is cold outside. As Moran writes, the spirit in which he presents his words is not, "'Now I have spoken; make of it what you will' but rather 'Take it from me'."[102] Consequently, relating to all tellings as evidence misconstrues the fact that the distinctive feature of testimony is that the speaker's telling is not data waiting for interpretation, but *assurance* for the truth of the statement. Moran therefore

---

[100] Gelfert, *Critical Introduction*, 163–179. [101] Moran, "Getting Told," 2.
[102] Moran, "Getting Told," 26.

describes the epistemic phenomenon of telling as an aspect of a "basic *relationship* between people."[103]

Importantly, assurance and evidential relations involve distinctly different logics of justification. Relating to something as a piece of evidence, I do not think of it as a message intentionally aimed at me. Moran illustrates this relation with a characteristic detective story scenario. The murderer did not leave a piece of evidence at the crime scene in order to make me believe something or other. Or rather, if he did, it constitutes "tainted" evidence:

> Ordinarily, if I confront something as evidence (the telltale footprint, the cigarette butt left in the ashtray) and then learn that it was left there deliberately, even with the intention of bringing me to a particular belief, this will only discredit it as evidence in my eyes. It won't seem better evidence, or even just as good, but instead like something fraudulent, or tainted evidence.[104]

This explicates a qualitative difference between two epistemic attitudes: one can relate to testimony *either* as assurance *or* as evidence. When articulating this contrast, Moran points out that if I see someone's testimony under the aspect of the concept of evidence, I should focus on unintended messages, that is, the speaker blushing, stammering or otherwise revealing that she has something to hide. Should she attempt to influence my opinion, then this would come out as manipulative. In contrast, if I relate to something in the spirit of assurance, then precisely the fact that the speaker wants to tell me something, and wants me to believe it, is a reason for me to believe him: "What this provides me with is different in kind, though not necessarily in degree of certainty."[105] Consequently, the two epistemic attitudes involve different logics of justification. What takes the appearance of support in the case of assurance, amounts to disproof in the case of evidence.

3.4 The Limits of the Evidential Paradigm

How does historical research relate to the difference between the epistemic attitudes of assurance and evidence? Facing this question, several cracks emerge in the evidential paradigm. First, it should be obvious that historians are not always only interested in the unintended evidence of testimony but also in the intended content. In such cases, Moran's distinction between different logics of justification holds also for historiography. The fact that a historical agent intentionally tells something, and wants his interlocutors to believe him, does not automatically make his statements fraudulent evidence. This implies

---

[103] Moran, "Getting Told," 2.   [104] Moran, "Getting Told," 6.   [105] Moran, "Getting Told," 6.

that one central claim of the evidential paradigm in historiography – that testimony is evidence *simpliciter* – is misleading. Contrary to non-intentional source material, such as minutes, train tickets and legal codes, the fact that testimony is produced with the explicit intent to convey certain information about the past does not diminish its credibility as proof. Of course, testimony is still treated as evidence for answering the historian's questions, which involves a demand for corroboration from other testimony and non-intentional material, but it is nonetheless treated distinctly *as a candidate for truth* (assurance) and not as mere data awaiting interpretation. In this sense, testimony is an epistemic source like no other in historiography.

The solidity of the evidential paradigm is challenged also by the fact that historians inevitably rely on tellings as assurance in their work. No researcher, historian or other, can possibly verify all the sources they rely on first-hand. Furthermore, the idea that historians could possibly relate to *all* tellings from historical agents as merely unintended evidence is incoherent. As Bloch and Collingwood emphasized, a central part of modern historical research is to interpret testimony in spite of itself. Especially Collingwood, who tended to be much more assertive on this issue than Bloch, claimed that such interpretations belong to the very essence of history. The scientific historian, Collingwood wrote, is "twisting a passage ostensibly about something different into an answer to the question he has decided to ask."[106] In other words, to do history *is* to draw conclusions about what a particular statement betrays about, say, cultural norms or the (hidden) motives of the agents. Still, it is not even logically possible that historians would always only read testimony against the grain. The impossibility of relating to statements by historical agents only as the evidence of unintended messages is obvious also in Bloch's classical example of reading Saint-Simon's statements as evidence of court mentality.[107]

If historians want to use statements in spite of themselves, they must first identify what the speakers are doing with their words. This identification is, as such, not independent from questions about the truth of the agent's statements. The question of truth is, however, not answered by Rankean gazing at the past. Rather, one evaluates the agent's statements as intentional messages in relation to other statements and our general knowledge of the context. Only this assessment will allow one to identify what Saint-Simon is, plausibly, doing with his words: is he telling, joking, guessing or reciting? Without this basic identification of the speech acts, one will not be able to make claims about the behavioural evidence of Saint-Simon's statements either. Clearly, any judgement about what kind of mentality Saint-Simon is inadvertently expressing will be dependent on

---

[106] Collingwood, *Idea of History*, 270.   [107] Bloch, *Historian's Craft*, 52–53.

whether one can identify when Saint-Simon is speaking sincerely and when he is not. One should, of course, not deny that these different aspects of Saint-Simon's statements are often mutually intertwined. Thus, understanding the mentality expressed in Saint-Simon's statements may also be crucial for correctly understanding his speech acts.

If *all* material of the past were treated merely as behavioural evidence, then historians could not get any foothold in their material to begin with. Held strictly within an (behavioural) evidential paradigm, the historian would be limited to making claims about the possible material causes of the remains from the past. Accordingly, historians would be limited to suppositions about whether the author of the source material was left-handed, perhaps a quill pen was used, and that one can see signs of stress in the handwriting and so forth. It is only by *not* relating to source material as behavioural evidence, but also as tellings offering assurance, that the credibility of the historical agent's original tellings can be examined. Often enough it may also be precisely the truth of the statements, rather than their status as cultural evidence, that interests the historian.

The evidential paradigm is misleading to the extent that it implies that testimony *qua* assurance has no role to play at all in historiography. Assurances are a central epistemic source also in historical research. In everything from everyday conversations to scientific research, one may relate to the tellings of others *either* as assurances, that is, as candidates for truth, *or* as (behavioural) evidence from which one arrives at one's own conclusions. As such, this distinction does show that Collingwood's exclamation that history has "no relation to testimony at all"[108] is an overstatement – if read as a denial of testimony as assurance in historical research. Acknowledging the role of assurance implies that this Element advances a mitigated form of evidentialism, in contrast with the austere evidentialism that some of Collingwood's and Bloch's claims seem to imply.[109]

3.5 Assurance and Epistemic Justification

It is not obvious that classical philosophers of history, such as Collingwood and Bloch, were indeed rejecting testimony as assurance from historical research. What they certainly rejected, as I will argue next, was, instead, that a historical agent's assurance *alone* can serve as epistemic justification for historical knowledge. In this respect, the question of testimony in historical research connects, again, with a much-debated issue in the recent epistemology of testimony: Is testimony an independent form of knowledge, or does it, in the end, require

---

[108] Collingwood, *Idea of History*, 203.
[109] I owe the term "mitigated evidentialism" to one of the anonymous reviewers of this Element.

validation from evidence? Answering this question, it will be pertinent to situate the case of historiography in relation to one of the most debated arguments for non-reductive testimonial knowledge; namely, the so-called Interpersonal View of Testimony (IVT).[110]

Several influential exponents of the IVT have argued that the justification of testimonial knowledge comes from the relationship of trust between the interlocutors. According to Benjamin McMyler, testimony provides justification by way of "the particular kind of reason that it does in virtue of the interpersonal relationship between us."[111] Or, as Edward Hinchman states, telling involves an invitation to trust.[112] Every time you tell me something, you want me to believe it because you said it, and my belief follows from our relation of trust. According to Paul Faulkner, the relationship of trust between the interlocutors is in itself "a reason providing state. . . . [O]ne where an audience (as truster) expects a speaker (as trusted) to try to say what is true because the audience is dependent on the speaker doing so."[113] The relationship of trust, therefore, is a kind of social fact that pushes people towards truthfulness in their communication with others. Thus, trusting someone for the truth implies that the listener has the right to resent the speaker in the event of cheating.[114] Conversely, the speaker who invites the audience to trust what she says is entitled to feel slighted if her words are not received as trust-based reasons for belief.[115] Thereby, telling creates obligations. In the paradigm case, I ought to expect my interlocutor to tell me the truth and I have the right to resent her if she does not.

The IVT is much debated in the contemporary epistemology of testimony. The central problem is: Why would the ethical and social dimensions of interpersonal relationships validate, or even make it probable, that my informant is *not* misleading me? How can the social and ethical facts of testimonial reliance be translated into epistemic warrant? Naturally, the proponents of the IVT do not want to suggest that we should always trust people when they tell us something. Considering this unclarity about the epistemic dimension, Jennifer Lackey argues that the IVT does not succeed in showing that knowledge from testimony is a separate, independent form of knowledge. Testimony is indeed a source of knowledge, but as data, and it is subject to all the tests that otherwise apply to data. As Lackey writes:

> [T]he proponent of the IVT faces a dilemma: either the view of testimony in question is genuinely interpersonal but epistemologically impotent, or it is not epistemologically impotent but neither is it genuinely interpersonal.

---

[110] Cf. Leonard, "Problems of Testimony." [111] McMyler, *Testimony*, 134.
[112] Hinchman, "Inviting to Trust." [113] Faulkner, "Telling and Trusting," 881.
[114] McMyler, *Testimony*, 127–128. [115] Hinchman, "Inviting to Trust," 566.

> Either way, the IVT fails to provide a compelling alternative to existing [evidentialist] theories in the epistemology of testimony.[116]

In other words, we trust testimony, not on the mere authority of the speaker, but because we have independent grounds. Trust does not solve the problem, because we must explain why we should trust the speaker. This means that, in the end, the epistemic justification of testimonial reliance is explained only by evidentialism.[117] This Element is not, however, the place for a detailed account of the debate about the IVT in the epistemology of testimony. Instead, I will use the problems identified for the IVT to explicate the role of justification from testimony in historical research. As I will show, the problems concerning the independent status of testimony as epistemic justification are further accentuated in historical research.

3.6 Communal Historiographic Argumentation

For the IVT, the concept of interpersonal trust explains why testimony can function as an independent form of knowledge. Typically, there is no such interpersonal relation of trust between the historian and historical agents. Already this fundamental difference implies that testimony cannot have the same justificatory role of providing assurance in the case of history. This difference is, however, not only because people in the past have not given historians their word. Even if a historical witness did give the historian his word, this does not mean that the historian, therefore, is related to the statement of the witness in the same way as in everyday conversations. The crucial difference is, of course, that historiography is a distinct research practice, while everyday conversations are not. Consequently, when the historical agent's assurances enter historiography, they become, by definition, subject to a space of contestation and argumentation. This fundamental space of historiographic argumentation was described by Ludwig Wittgenstein as "the historical proof game."[118] Collingwood, in turn, used a similar metaphor:

> [W]hen one takes up the study of some difficult historical question, ... there is one thing which one cannot fail to observe. This is the existence of what I may call the rules of the game. One rule – the first – runs thus: 'You must not say anything, however true, for which you cannot produce evidence.' The game is won not by the player who can reconstitute what really happened, but by the player who can show that his view of what happened is the one which

---

[116] Lackey, *Knowing from Words*, 222.
[117] Lackey, *Knowing from Words*, 230–232, 239–240.
[118] Wittgenstein, *Culture and Value*, 32.

the evidence accessible to all players, when criticised up to the hilt, supports.[119]

Today, Collingwood's view about the rules of the game – which he later calls the definition of historical thinking – is very much in line with a broad explanationist consensus about proof in historiography. Explanationism stresses that all knowledge is relative to specific epistemic contexts, fallible, and assumes a hypothetical character – there is no foundation for knowledge claims beyond the ways in which the game of proof is played within the community of professional historical research. In this spirit, Lorenz has argued that "The problem of justification in philosophy of history boils down to the question of what kinds of argumentation historians use to argue their claims to knowledge."[120] A similar focus on justification through argumentation is found among many theorists writing about historical evidence and proof today.[121]

The metaphor of games and players is very appropriate since it turns our attention towards the communal nature of historiography.[122] Because history is communal, the historian must appeal to independently ascertainable grounds when arguing about whether a testimonial account should be accepted. Appealing to independent grounds entails a conceptual shift in one's relation to the word of others. As Collingwood phrases the change: "As soon as there are such grounds, the case is no longer one of testimony."[123] If one is appealing to grounds available to everyone, then one is, in fact, no longer accepting something merely based on one's own relation of trust to the person offering testimony.

The crucial role of communal reasoning also explains why the model of inheriting justification, sometimes called epistemic buck passing, cannot serve as an argument for testimonial reliance in historiography.[124] This argument, endorsed by Mark Day, claims that testimony is to be viewed not as a transmission of knowledge but as a transmission of justification. As Day writes:

> [A]cceptance [of testimony] should be regarded as a matter of inheriting the justification that the testifier possessed; it cannot be a matter of treating the testimony as evidence that invites further reasoning. If that is correct, then if S tells you what they have seen and you believe them, then your belief is as

---

[119] Collingwood, "Limits of Historical Knowledge," 97.
[120] Lorenz, "Historical Knowledge," 307.
[121] See Day, *Philosophy of History*; Kuukkanen; *Postnarrativist*; Kosso, "Historical Evidence"; Goldstein, *Philosophical Essays*; Tucker, *Knowledge of the Past*; Murphey, *Truth and History*; Tamm, "Truth."
[122] In this respect, historiography shares the social character of all scientific research. For contemporary discussion in the philosophy of science, see Oreskes, *Why Trust Science?*
[123] Collingwood, *Idea of History*, 257.   [124] McMyler, *Testimony*, 61–65.

directly justified by S's observation as S's belief is. This argument doesn't commit one to the obviously false claim that all testimony is justified; only that, where it is, the recipient's justification is the same as the testifier.[125]

Day is right concerning justification for the content of the belief, but he underestimates the difference the communal nature of historiography makes for the transmission of justification. To engage in historical research *is* to engage in a critical practice that invites further reasoning about why some testimony should be accepted. As we saw, this does not mean testimony reduces to behavioural evidence in historiography, but it means that the historian's reason for accepting a statement is necessarily related to grounds in a way that acceptance of the word of a friend in everyday conversations is not. In the case of friendship, my personal relationship to my friend *is* my grounds. Not only that I may accept my friend's word because of our friendship, but also that in relation to the word of my friend there is normally no doubt that needs grounds to be defeated. The default position in history, however, is different. When questions are raised about reliability, testimony is always-already in need of independent grounds to convince *other historians* of the reasonability of its acceptance.

Contrary to everyday conversations, historians must always appeal to grounds beyond their own relationship to the events or persons involved. For instance, historians are already appealing to something independently available by claiming that someone is a trustworthy witness. Such claims are inevitably connected with producing arguments, available to the community of historians, for why one should consider someone reliable. But to say that I take someone's word because they have been shown to be reliable is no longer simply to accept something on another person's say-so. By appealing to someone's trustworthiness, I am, in essence, relying on independent grounds, available to everyone, and not merely accepting that person's word. I have, in fact, reasoned independently and come to the conclusion that, on this subject, it is reasonable to accept that person's statement. In addition, historians are only justified in such reasoning if they can convince their colleagues that they too would have come to the same conclusion. The leap to something independently acceptable, which historical research necessarily involves, entails that testimony cannot have the same justificatory role as it may have in everyday conversations. For the historian, contrary to everyday conversations, all transmission of justification is subject to the communal process of historiographic argumentation.

In sum, it is important to explicate and sometimes moderate the conceptual rejection of testimony in modern history. Historical research does indeed share the basic dependence on testimony that fundamentally shapes knowledge

---

[125] Day, *Philosophy of History*, 206, 48.

acquisition in all sciences and everyday life. But there are also significant differences. The impossibility of deferring responsibility derives from the communal nature of historical research, which implies that reasons for belief are subject to a collegial argumentative process. Nevertheless, historians do not relate to testimony only as evidence in the sense of data to be interpreted, but also as assurances with intentional content, offering candidates for truth. Concerning the epistemic dimension of testimony in historiography, it is very important to avoid dualism: historiography involves relating to the words of witnesses *both* as evidence and as assurance, and these distinct epistemic attitudes are not mutually exclusive.

The entire discussion has so far focused on the relation between testimony and historical facts. The main point of comparison was knowledge and belief acquisition in the epistemology of testimony in general, and particularly the role of non-reductive testimonial knowledge in historiography. This framework is, however, useful only for the limited yet important aspect of establishing singular propositional facts in historiography. Furthermore, (analytic) epistemology of testimony is often labouring under a fundamental presupposition that historiography does not always share. One assumes that the speaker knows what the hearer wants to know, and that the task is to investigate how the transmission of knowledge between the interlocutors is possible.[126] As we already saw, however, seminal philosophers of history have argued that historiography involves a distinct form of understanding that goes beyond the knowledge and understanding of events that historical witnesses could possibly have had. In fact, Danto considered going beyond the understanding of historical witnesses as the distinctive feature of historiography. This contention – which became formative for narrativist philosophy of history – was articulated in Danto's account of the historian's narrative sentences. Historiography, Danto argued, necessarily involves describing past actions and events in retrospective terms that were (logically) unavailable to contemporaries. His by now famous example was "The Thirty Years' War started in 1618."[127] It is to the relation between historical understanding and testimony that this Element must turn next.

4 Testimony, Understanding and Ethics

In recent historical theory, discussions about testimony have focused on the ways in which memory accounts relate to historical understanding.[128] These discussions

---

[126] This assumption is sometimes called the "Content Preservation Model," see Pollock, "Testimonial Knowledge."
[127] Danto, *Analytical Philosophy of History*, 143–183.
[128] See, for example, Spiegel, "Future of the Past," 175–177; Tozzi, "Role of Testimony," 12–15; Jenkins, "Ethical Responsibility," 55; Assman, "History, Memory."

have, at least, two major themes. First, it has been argued that both history and memory offer forms of understanding that are equally conditioned by language as well as politics, culture and identity. This shared predicament, accentuated by the linguistic turn in history, has motivated a general rapprochement between historical research and testimony. As a result, testimony is, Aleida Assmann writes, "advancing from a rival to a partner of historiography."[129] Second, the inclusion of testimony has been framed as not only legitimate but also important for an ethical understanding of the past within historiographical discourse. The ethical contribution of witness testimony to historical research lies, allegedly, in the authentic experiential dimension of the events that it transmits to the receiver.

This section places the recent embrace of testimony in historical theory – specifically as a vehicle for transmitting experience and understanding – in dialogue with classical work in the philosophy of history about the conceptual distinctiveness of historical understanding. Centrally, this task involves situating the claim for testimony in historiography in relation to the fundamental conceptual distinction between the historical and the practical past. Although this distinction has been discussed abundantly in the wake of Hayden White's *The Practical Past*, this Element constitutes one of the first explicit efforts to put the distinction to work for understanding the relation between testimony and historical research.[130] The distinction itself hails, of course, from the philosophy of Oakeshott.[131]

The section starts with a brief presentation of the rebirth of testimony in historiography in 4.1. The two following subsections, 4.2–4.3, present and criticize recent attempts to either subsume history under the conceptual umbrella of cultural memory, or to reduce history to practical knowledge by appealing to the historicity of historiography itself. In 4.4–4.5, I present my alternative to these views by mobilizing Oakeshott's philosophy in support of the autonomy of historical understanding in relation to testimony and memory. Thereafter, in 4.6–4.7, I use this idea of autonomy for a critique of recent attempts to harmonize testimony and historical understanding. Finally, in 4.8, I argue that the ethics of history is not reducible to the ethics of practical relations to the past, which means that the historian's concern for ethics cannot be outsourced to testimony.

4.1 The Rebirth of Testimony in Historiography

The 1970s brought revolutionary changes for the role of testimony in historical research. Naturally, the use of testimony as evidence for establishing facts carried on as before, but there was undoubtedly also a distinctly new kind of

---

[129] Assman, "History, Memory," 261.
[130] This section develops my earlier work on the topic, see my "Testimony Stops."
[131] For a discussion of White's and Oakeshott's diverging uses of the distinction, see my "Michael Oakeshott and Hayden White."

interest in testimony. The subjectivity of witness accounts, which was considered a central weakness in the nineteenth-century turn to scientific history, rose up as the main strength of testimonial material. This turn involves focusing on the *how* rather than on the *what* of witness accounts – the truth of the telling rather than the telling of the truth. Using Christopher Browning's distinction, historians became interested in the "authenticity" of testimony rather than merely their "factual accuracy," or lack thereof.[132] As Assmann writes, this new contribution of testimony is framed not as a pathway to objective facts, but rather as the royal road to authentic experience: "Their point is less to tell us what happened than what it felt like to be in the center of those events; they provide very personal views from within."[133] With this shift of interest, it was not uncommon for testimony to be assigned the role of an immediate link to the past, transmitting directly the emotional and experiential dimension of historical events, especially concerning the so-called limit events of the twentieth century.[134]

Today, testimony is a major topic in many fields of the humanities – from gender studies to analytic epistemology and phenomenology – and the interdisciplinary field of testimony studies has grown exponentially since the 1980s.[135] One overarching development is, of course, the rise of interest in experience, memory and subjectivity within all the humanities. For historiography, this turn was originally fuelled primarily by democratic aspirations of creating counter-narratives "from below," but memory has moved from being an alternative, minority movement to becoming the hegemonic form of popular historical representation. Some scholars even claim that professional historians have lost their positions as the go-to interpreters of the collective past. At least in public domains, historians are increasingly replaced by eyewitness accounts of those "who were there when it actually happened," as stylishly framed by journalists, authors, documentary producers, game designers and museum curators.[136] As Sara Jones has argued, the appeal of testimony is closely connected with the idea that eyewitnesses can offer historical understanding something unique (a [perceived] authentic account of the past), thus relying on "the sense that [witnesses] must know what it was like because they were there and the promise that this experience can be transmitted to the listener, reader, visitor or viewer."[137]

---

[132] Browning, *Remembering Survival*, 8. [133] Assman, "History, Memory," 263.
[134] See Tozzi, "Role of Testimony," 4–5; Hutton, *Art of Memory*.
[135] For up-to-date reviews of this development, see Jones and Woods, "Testimony in Culture"; Krämer and Weigel, "Converging Testimony Studies," ix–xli; and Kilby and Rowland, *Future of Testimony*.
[136] Sabrow, "Der Zeitzeuge," 20–22. [137] Jones, "Mediated Immediacy," 136.

In historiography, the new interest in testimony connects with two concurrent scholarly and popular trends: the rise of victim testimony and the politics of identity. For the former, it is widely acknowledged that the rise of victim testimony is inextricably linked to the process of relating to witness accounts from Holocaust survivors, which was set in motion in the wake of the Eichmann trials in the 1960s. This process inspired a massive upsurge of both public and scholarly interest in memory accounts, a turn that the French historian Annette Wieviorka has labelled the advent of an "Era of the Witness."[138] This characterization is not peculiar to Wieviorka; many influential scholars have acknowledged the turn toward memory accounts for understanding events in the collective past. For instance, Jay Winter has written that memory is "the historical signature of our own generation," Pierre Nora has claimed that our time is an "era of commemoration," and Kerwin Lee Klein has argued that memory has become the dominating metaphor for understanding how the present should come to terms with the collective past.[139]

The turn toward memory accounts is closely connected with the politics of identity. As Nora argued, there are as many advocates of memory accounts of past events as there are collective groups in society.[140] This claim is well-supported by the fact that memory accounts typically serve as instruments for advancing the status of group identities. In many cases, articulating the experiences of oppression through testimony is tantamount to a claim for the acknowledgement of a particular group identity. The American historian Allan Megill proposed a formula for highlighting this connection: "Where identity is problematized, memory is valorized."[141] Furthermore, this development is often linked with an ethically motivated idea of multiperspectivity. Memory and testimony give researchers access to the counter-stories of historically disadvantaged communities, stories that can be used to criticize hegemonic narratives and highlight subalternity.[142] Consequently, accounts from memory have become a central tool for writing histories about experiences that had previously been either simply avoided or downright silenced.[143]

4.2 The Culturalist Challenge to History

The comprehensive turn towards testimony and memory has been labelled "one of the main challenges in the theory and practice of history in the recent few decades."[144] The rebirth of testimony, it is argued, entails that previously upheld

---

[138] Wieviorka, *Era of the Witness*.
[139] Winter, "Generation of Memory"; Nora, "Era of Commemoration"; Klein, "Emergence of Memory."
[140] Nora, "Memory and History." [141] Megill, "History, Memory, Identity," 40.
[142] Forcinito, "Testimonio"; Abu-Lughod and Sa'di, "Introduction."
[143] See Cubitt, "History of Memory." [144] Tamm, "Memory," 544.

oppositions between historical understanding and memory accounts should be dismantled. Both history and testimony offer ways to understand historical events, and both are equally conditioned by linguistic and cultural mediation as well as present concerns of politics, power and identity.[145] Thus, historical writing can be subsumed under the metaphor of memory and characterized as but one of many cultural vehicles for collectively remembering the past in the present. As the debates about history and memory can fill a small library, the following will focus only on features especially relevant for the specificity of historical understanding in contrast with understanding the past via testimony.[146] There are, of course, also several notable critics of the ongoing general rapprochement between history and memory.[147]

For the case of testimony, the most popular method of rapprochement is to subsume history under the category of culture. This leads to the conclusion that academic history is just one among many cultural practices for relating to the past. As we have seen, memory and history have traditionally been viewed as opposites ever since the advent of the Rankean paradigm. Memory was downgraded as subjective, unreliable and partial, whereas history has been placed on an epistemic pedestal as objective, reliable and universal. Drawing on work in memory studies, especially Peter Burke, Aleida and Jan Assmann, and Patrick Hutton, Marek Tamm has argued for overcoming this opposition by viewing historiography itself as a culturally specific memory practice in its own time. As Burke proposed, one may treat historiography "much as Halbwachs treated memory, as the product of social groups such as Roman senators, Chinese mandarins, Benedictine monks, university professors, and so on."[148]

In brief, Tamm proposes a "solution" to the opposition between memory and history by arguing that "history is a cultural form exactly like, for instance, religion, literature, art, or myth, all of which contribute to the production of cultural memory."[149] According to Tamm, however, the reduction of historical writing to cultural memory does not spell the end of history's "scientific pretensions."[150] Historiography is still a very specific medium of cultural memory with its own rules and traditions, including documentary evidence and professional critique.[151] The consequence of the reduction is, instead, that one must reject "the illusion" of a "determined, fixed historical past, lying

---

[145] For arguments in this direction, see Burke, "History as Social Memory"; Bourke, "'Remembering' War"; Assmann, "Transformations," and Tamm, "Beyond History."
[146] For overviews, see Cubitt, "History of Memory" and Confino, "History and Memory."
[147] For example, Megill, "History, Memory, Identity"; Kansteiner, "Finding Meaning"; Barash, *Cultural Memory*.
[148] Burke quoted in Tamm, "Memory," 548.   [149] Tamm, "Memory," 549.
[150] Tamm, "Beyond History," 463.
[151] Tamm, "Beyond History," 463; Tamm, "Memory," 549.

beyond the pale of living memory and clearly distinct from our present concerns."[152] What one must accept is that history writing is one among many "memorial activities" in which individuals and groups "recollect and construe the past selectively through various media."[153]

This argument is as correct as it is irrelevant. Of course, historiography *can* be viewed as a specific cultural form. The professional historian was certainly well represented as a producer of cultural memory during the heyday of European nationalism.[154] Still, this culturalist argument is completely beside the point for understanding the conceptual distinctiveness of historiography in relation to testimony. Without pausing, Tamm contends that "in terms of cultural memory, history is a cultural form."[155] This is obviously true, but Tamm provides no argument whatsoever for why it would be sufficient to consider historiography only in terms of cultural memory in the first place.

For instance, one may consider Ludwig Wittgenstein's *Tractatus Logico-Philosophicus* (1922) in cultural terms as an expression of late Viennese Fin-de-siècle literature. This is, however, only one way to understand the work. In contrast, one may understand the *Tractatus* as philosophy and engage directly with the conceptual questions that the work poses about logic, language and reality. Certainly, the same goes for historiography. One may relate to historiography *either* as a cultural practice *or* as a philosophical idea with distinct presuppositions, principles and a priori concepts. While it is true that *qua* cultural practice historiography may serve the same function of cultural memory as witness literature or myth, this says nothing yet about the conceptual relation between testimony and historiography as forms of thought about the past. In other words, the only thing Tamm's solution to the opposition between memory and history offers is a description of what historiography looks like from the viewpoint of a cultural historian. One can, and should, proceed to consider the relation from the perspective of philosophy and the theory of history.

4.3 The Historicity of History

Philosophically more astute, although similar in content, is the argument for rapprochement considering that historiography is, like testimony, always-already framed by the historian's own, present historical situation. This argument for the historicity of history, hailing at least from Walter Benjamin, takes many different forms but all of them reject a simple binary between history and memory.[156] For example, Dominick LaCapra and Paul Ricoeur reject the binary

---

[152] Tamm, "Memory," 549.   [153] Tamm, "Memory," 549–550.
[154] Berger and Lorenz, *Nationalizing the Past*.   [155] Tamm, "Memory," 549.
[156] For the relation to Benjamin, see Baquero, "Memory, Narrative."

because history grows out of cultural memory and relations of transference, María-Inés Mudrovcic because "historical time" can no longer be separated from the present, and Mark Day because historiography depends on the historian's multiple relations to the past.[157] The postmodern revelation that history is constructed in the present, Assmann argues, persuades one to accept that "history is itself a form of memory."[158] In essence, these scholars pose the question: Can the historian's relation to the past ever be strictly a historical one? In other words, is the ideal of question-driven rational reasoning from evidence, which is the cornerstone of the evidential paradigm in historical research, really an apt description of what an individual historian's relation to the past looks like in real life? And where does the motive for engaging in historical research come from?

This reality check, so to speak, is especially relevant considering recent work in historical theory. Influential theorists have shown how past actions and events refuse to become the dead historical past of evidence, and instead returns in experience and claims for justice and recognition in the present.[159] As a result, the evidential paradigm, along with the focus on narrative form, has recently been problematized as a narrow and one-dimensional understanding of the historian's relation to the past. Instead, many historical theorists have argued for approaches that highlight the multifarious relations between historians and the past that they investigate.[160] According to Mark Day, who invented the "relations with the past" notion, the main concern for twenty-first century historical theory should be to assess how epistemic issues in history are entangled with relations to the past that he calls "evaluative, preservative, dialogic, material and practical."[161] These relations are inseparably connected with the epistemology of history, and the latter cannot be properly understood without taking the former into account.[162]

The relations Day speaks about are not principally a matter of choice but relations every historian enters into by the mere fact of inhabiting a world inherited from previous generations. This feature is most clear with the relations he calls material and practical: we begin our lives with artefacts from the past already in place and conventional (practical) ways of relating to events in the past. The "evaluative," "preservative" and "dialogical" relations are similarly

---

[157] Ricoeur, *Memory, History, Forgetting*; LaCapra, *History and Memory*; Mudrovcic, "Time, History," *History of the Present Time*; Day, *Philosophy of History*.
[158] Assmann, "Transformations," 62.
[159] Ankersmit, *Sublime Historical*; Bevernage, "Time, Presence"; *State-Sponsored Violence*; Kleinberg, *Haunting History*; Runia, *Moved by the Past*. See also, Lorenz and Bevernage, *Breaking Up Time*.
[160] Paul, *Key Issues*.   [161] Day, "Relations with the Past," 418.
[162] Day, "Relations with the Past," 419–424.

not a matter of choice for the historian but part of the conditions for acquiring historical knowledge at all. The evaluative concerns the necessity of selection and thick descriptions in history, the preservative is about the historian's basic reliance on testimony and the dialogical is the possibility of being challenged by voices from the past in historical interpretation. As LaCapra has argued, such challenges are vital for articulating the historian's subject-position.[163] Without the opportunity to be challenged by testimony, it would be impossible for the historian to attain a reflective relation to the ways in which their own preconceptions may lead to epistemic and hermeneutic injustice.[164]

The argument for multiple relations with the past in historiography is important. Every historiographical work will inevitably start from the individual historian's historically determined, multifarious relations with the past. For example, the practical dimension is evident already in the historian's choice of what testimony to use as evidence. As is well-known from the history of historical research, much testimony was not even considered relevant source material for doing history until the turn toward history "from below" in the 1960s. The fact that women, workers and subaltern subjects are indeed also historical agents became obvious for historians only gradually. In this respect, every historiographical work will be shaped by the individual historian's practical relations to the past. For example, the concern for neglected and silenced subjects may serve as crucial input concerning what testimony historians analyze in their professional work. Undoubtedly, historians may even consider it as part of their ethical responsibility to also use previously neglected testimony as evidence in their research. Consequently, the ethical aspect of the historian's choices *prior* to their research work implies an important connection between historical research and the practical past.

4.4 The Ideal Past of History

Does the historicity of history imply that the conceptual distinction between the historical and practical past collapses? No, but it highlights that precision is needed for appreciating the import of the distinction. The purpose of the distinction, at least for Oakeshott, was not to provide empirical categories within which actual historiography can be placed into boxes as either historical or practical. If this were the case, then the distinction would indeed collapse since no historian can escape practical relations to the past completely.[165] Instead, the historical and the practical is an ideal-type distinction similar in

---

[163] LaCapra, *History and Memory*, 40. See also my "Crisis of Testimony."
[164] Fricker, *Epistemic Injustice*.
[165] My earlier work on Oakeshott did not fully appreciate this point. See my "Michael Oakeshott and Hayden White."

kind to, for example, Aristotle's distinction between six forms of political constitution.[166] For the latter, the types of constitution are not descriptive of existing ancient Greek states but denote rather the logical possibilities of political organization. Consequently, Aristotle's principles of classification between *poleis* ruled by one, a few, or by many, do not become useless simply from the fact they do not correspond with Greek political experience, and arguably no state could ever be ruled by one person alone. The purpose of the distinction was, instead, to philosophically explicate the internal tendencies towards stability or instability, justice or injustice, within logically distinct ideal types of political constitution. Recently, Martyn P. Thompson has argued lucidly for an ideal-type interpretation of Oakeshott's distinction. He writes:

> [J]ust as Aristotle's 'monarchy,' say, as an ideal type of constitution is not an actual monarchy, Oakeshott's ideal mode of historical understanding is not an actual history. Instead, it is the logically coherent ideal type of historical understanding that allows an observer to discern what the constituent elements of understanding are that are implicit within and exclusive to genuinely historical accounts of the past. These are the constituent elements by virtue of which those accounts can be and are recognized as historical accounts (more or less; in part or in full), rather than accounts of different, non-historical kinds like myths, legends, propaganda or historical fiction.[167]

Consequently, the fact that individual historians always have multiple relations to the past is not a problem for the conceptual distinction between historical and practical past. Just like every existing monarchy, all historiographical work will inevitably be the product of many different historical and social circumstances – historians may even understand their own work as interventions in such circumstances. Regardless of this fact, however, it will still be possible to isolate and discern the ways in which ideal-type elements are present within the real-life existing empirical cases of historiography. In other words, the fact that historiography will always harbour several different relations to the past does not spell the end for the (logical) possibility of autonomy and critical knowledge about the past.

In Oakeshott's philosophy of history, the practical and the historical denote different (ideal) conceptual spaces. This means that "the practical" and "the historical" do not refer to different past realms but to different kinds of constructions of present evidence. The practical and the historical past are, respectively, produced by attending to material from the past via either a practical or a historical mode of understanding. In this context, the term "history" is used as

---

[166] For the general importance of ideal-type concepts in historical theory, see Paul, *Key Issues*.
[167] Thompson, *Oakeshott*, 38.

a term of art. For Oakeshott (and Collingwood), history is a specific form of understanding and not, as in everyday usage, a word synonymous with a specific temporal location, the past. Consequently, to say that testimony is not historical, as both Oakeshott and Collingwood would, is not to deny that testimony may be from the past, nor that testimony is conditioned by past circumstances. Rather, not historical means not the product of historical forms of understanding.[168]

If past material becomes the focus of our practical understanding, then a practical past is created. In such cases, and testimony is a good example, we are concerned with "the past" for the sake of the present and the future. The practical past is, by definition, a past that is not thought of as worth knowing for its own sake but only "in relation to ourselves and our current activities."[169] We use this kind of past "to make valid practical beliefs about the present and the future."[170] This practical past is everywhere available and consists of the "accumulation of symbolic persons, actions, utterances, situations and artefacts," which Oakeshott regarded as an "indispensable ingredient of an articulate civilized life."[171] By contrast, the historical past is a past that is thought to exist independently of our own concerns. The past of history is studied for its own sake and deserves investigation in its own right.[172]

4.5 Autonomy Is Not Impartiality

Does the seeming commitment to own sake-ism expose "the historical past" as simply a sophisticated, covert argument for the old Rankean ideal of impartial and objective history? In other words, is the argument for autonomy an argument for impartiality?[173] For clarifying this issue, it is worth-while considering how Collingwood – who considered Oakeshott's philosophy of history a "highwater mark" – responded to the question of impartiality.[174] In his lecture to the *Stubbs Historical Society* in 1936, titled "Can Historians be Impartial?", Collingwood probably surprised his audience when he denied not only that impartiality is possible but also that it is even desirable. Collingwood argued:

> I see going on around me conscious attempts to study history from, say, a Communist point of view, setting out with the avowed intention of forcing upon it a particular interpretation. I applaud these attempts. The people who make them have seized on the great truth that all genuine historical thought begins with prejudice, and that people who deny this are either too stupid to

---

[168] For a discussion of this sense of "history," see my book *Primacy of Method*, 5–12.
[169] Oakeshott, *Rationalism in Politics*, 162.   [170] Oakeshott, *Experience and Its Modes*, 105.
[171] Oakeshott, *On History*, 44.   [172] Oakeshott, *On History*, 27.
[173] I am grateful to one of the anonymous reviewers for raising this specific question.
[174] Collingwood, *Idea of History*, 159. For a discussion of Collingwood's critique of Oakeshott's concept of historical past, see my book *Primacy of Method*, 88–93.

recognize their own prejudices or else ashamed to avow them. I agree that the so-called unprejudiced historical inquiry of orthodox historians falls between two stools: either it is riddled with national prejudice, class prejudice, the prejudice of a school of thought and so on, or else, in so far as it is really devoid of important prejudice, it is eunuch-history, written by people with no insight into its subject matter.[175]

In this quote, Collingwood sees partiality as the pervasive preconception and worldview we can never avoid. Our attempts to avoid partiality by disavowal or positioning are a futile struggle against a logical impossibility. No one can pull themselves up by their own bootstraps. Instead, we should realize that prejudice is, rather, a resource for the historian; it provides "steam in the engine of historical thought."[176] However, the attentive reader will notice a subtle distinction in Collingwood's quote. He is not saying that historical thought *is* prejudiced, but that historical thought *begins* from prejudice. The distinction is crucial.

Thinking historically, according to Collingwood's arguments in this lecture, means caring for the integrity of the past. Such care implies that historians are committed to the idea that past realities existed in their own right. As a result, there is always a question of whether our interpretations do justice to the past realities they deal with. Our interpretations and past realities are two different things – if we think about the past as historians and not as novelists. This fundamental distinction meant that Collingwood was not at all concerned about ideological interpretive frameworks in historical research. As long as we are still engaged in historical thinking, our prejudices will be broken and reshaped in the encounter with the source material. Collingwood enthusiastically claimed that "the power of historical thinking" makes him convinced that investigations carried out for political purposes also lead to historical results beyond mere ideological confirmation.[177]

One may not share Collingwood's optimism about the power of historical thinking to break the chains of prejudice.[178] The principal conceptual distinction at issue, however, is not affected by psychological factors. Although all historians are prejudiced, it will still be possible to conceptually distinguish between interpreting historical actions and events from the horizon of the past versus the horizon of the historian's present. It was that very conceptual

---

[175] Collingwood, *Principles of History*, 213. [176] Collingwood, *Principles of History*, 213.
[177] Collingwood, *Principles of History*, 213.
[178] The current so-called "New History Wars" provide ample reasons for being more sceptical than Collingwood was about the power of historical thought in relation to political divisions. See Frum, "New History Wars."

distinction that Oakeshott was articulating in his argument for the autonomy of historical thought.

Contrary to practical understanding, Oakeshott argued, the historical mode of understanding attends to material from the past as survivals to be treated "as evidence of past happenings."[179] The aim of this mode of understanding is to establish the "authentic meaning" of such remains in relation to the historian's questioning-activity.[180] On this view, history does not, contrary to what Mudrovcic and others suggest, rely on the absolute separation of historical time, but only on the reconstruction of a hypothetical past that explains the evidence.[181] The historical past should *not* be mistaken for a tool of temporal othering. Clearly, difference from the present is not a necessary condition for the historian's explanation of evidence.[182] The historical past is premised neither on the break between past and present, nor on gazing the material for "what really happened," but on constructing a picture of the past based on what present evidence obliges one to believe. In this process, the historical mode of understanding uses analytical concepts and narrative sentences to construct a past that never existed except in the writings of historians.[183] Consequently, it is also incorrect to equate the historical past, as Tamm suggested, with the idea of a forever determined and fixed past – unless one is fighting the ghost of Ranke. Nevertheless, the historical past is not an arbitrary construction but is based on the rational commitment to believe only what the evidence obliges. As Bernard Williams argued, belief aims at truth, and this means that historians can never legitimately decide to believe whatever they want about the past.[184]

The ideal-type interpretation of historical understanding is crucial for appreciating the relation between history and testimony. This interpretation allows for the carving out of an independent conceptual space for historical relations to the past. The conceptual space of history is one in which critique and evidential inference are, categorically, *not* employed for practical concerns in the present.[185] Oakeshott's original aim with his distinction was to show that the practical mode is not the only possible relation to the past.[186] In contrast, advocates for the rapprochement of testimony and history deny this very possibility. This is the essence of Tamm's culturalist argument as well as the arguments for history as (merely) a product of non-historical relations to the

---

[179] Oakeshott, *Rationalism in Politics,* 165.   [180] Oakeshott, *On History,* 38.
[181] Cf. Mudrovcic, "Time, History"; de Certeau, *Heterologies,* 215–217; Bevernage, *State-Sponsored Violence,* 5; Lorenz and Bevernage, *Breaking Up Time.*
[182] For further arguments in defence of this claim, see my *Primacy of Method,* 7–12.
[183] Oakeshott, *On History,* 32–33. Danto, *Analytical Philosophy of History.*
[184] Williams, "Deciding to Believe."
[185] For a penetrating discussion of this issue, see Thompson, *Oakeshott.*
[186] O'Sullivan, *Oakeshott,* 228.

past. The decisive fallacy here is to assume that *if* something is a construction in the present, *then* such constructions are all of the same kind.[187] This idea was aptly articulated by the oral historian Roseanne Kennedy:

> For once historians accept that all evidence is constructed – that it only becomes meaningful, and indeed, only functions as evidence, through particular discursive frameworks – then they must acknowledge that they, like witnesses, are meaning makers, not detectives or judges who 'find fact'. . . . [O]nly the culturally conferred status and authority of the historian distinguishes his or her interpretation of evidence from the interpretation found in testimonies.[188]

Oakeshott's distinction proves the contrary. He shows that it is conceptually possible – even within a thoroughly constructivist view of historical knowledge – to distinguish categorically between historical and practical modes of understanding past material. Consequently, arguing for the rapprochement of testimony and history based on the truism that "all evidence is constructed" is a non-starter. Not all constructions of meaning are of the same kind, and interpreting past material considering practical concerns in the present is not the only alternative available. Recognizing practical understanding as a specific perspective for understanding past material entails, ipso facto, that it is *not* the only perspective we can have. For acknowledging something as *a* perspective means that one can "make room for other modes of understanding."[189] In other words, embracing constructivism does not bring historical thinking closer to the understanding of the past found in testimonies.

4.6 The Claim of Testimony: Experience and Understanding

As we have seen, there are no compelling arguments for the rapprochement between historical understanding and testimony. Arguments for testimony in historiography need not, however, rely on the failed project of conceptual merger. Instead, one may argue for the inclusion of testimony on ethical grounds, justified theoretically by the consequences of the linguistic turn. Gabrielle M. Spiegel has summarized the result of this reasoning in an illuminating way:

> It does appear that . . . ethical claims for "justice" embedded in testimony and traumatic memory are sufficiently powerful to justify their admission into normal historiographical discourse, despite the notorious vagaries of memory, not to mention its culturally and socially mediated character. Yet to the extent that the "linguistic turn" has already modified our understanding of the truth

---

[187] For a critique of presentism, see Ahlskog and D'Oro, "Imagination and Revision."
[188] Kennedy, "Stolen Generations Testimony," 511.   [189] Oakeshott, *On History*, 26.

claims embedded in historical work and more or less laid to rest the notion of "objectivity" as an illusion, epistemological revisions to traditional historiographical pursuits have long been in place.... [T]he historian is as imbricated in the cultural and psychological forces at play in the construction of the past as the victim.[190]

Here, Spiegel is not claiming that historians and witnesses are on par epistemologically speaking. Rather, she is arguing that at stake is a question about "an ethical response to the catastrophes of the last century and ... a turn from epistemological to ethical commitments in the study of the past."[191] Consequently, the rapprochement between testimony and history is not about the epistemic dimension, or, in Spiegel's terms, the "responsibility to seek to 'get it right' in our investigations of the past."[192] Instead, it is in relation to conditions of understanding – the dimension of meaning – where history and memory come together.

Spiegel's account is nuanced. The argument is not that historiography and testimony are identical as forms of understanding either, but rather that their shared condition justifies the admission of the "ethical" understanding offered by memory accounts in "normal historiographical discourse." Considering that arguments for conceptual merger have already been dealt with, the following focuses on two other premises for including the "ethical" dimension of testimony in historiography. The first is the premise that the form of understanding that testimony offers is indeed relevant for, and compatible with, historiography, when the latter has been freed from objectivist pretensions. For investigating this premise, one must scrutinize the kind of understanding that testimony offers and how it relates to historical understanding. After that, I will consider the second premise; the idea that testimony offers a pertinent framework for articulating the ethics of historical research.

What exactly is the ethical and existential contribution to understanding that testimony offers historiography? The salient concepts in this discussion are authenticity, voice, experience, immediacy, trauma and embodied/existential truth – all of which are related to the often invoked but conceptually imprecise goal of understanding what it was like to live through certain historical events.[193] This very interest is, of course, related to the fact that almost all discussions are framed by victim testimony about so-called limit events that, by definition, pose the problem of understanding and representing extreme atrocities and genocide, among which the Holocaust is still the paradigm example.

---

[190] Spiegel, "Future of the Past," 177.   [191] Spiegel, "Future of the Past," 177.
[192] Spiegel, "Future of the Past," 177.
[193] For discussion of these debated terms, see Krämer, "Bearing Witness," 32–36; Jones, "Mediated Immediacy," 140–142; Jones, "Testimony through Culture," 262–264; Spiegel, "Future of the Past," 163–165, 175; and Saupe and Roche, "Testimonies in Historiography," 80–83. See also Cath, *What It Is Like*.

The contribution to understanding that testimony supposedly offers to history comes in two different forms. First, there is the idea that testimony offers unmediated access to the witnesses' experience. This is sometimes framed as the embodied or existential truth of a testimony.[194] From this perspective, the witness is to be interpreted *not* as someone transmitting a ready-made understanding in their representation of the events. Instead, much like a footprint in sand, one should relate to testimony not as a conscious representation but as an imprint of the event itself. This means that the words of the witness, and their silence (the void), testify directly to the events by way of the immediacy familiar from traumatic experiences.[195] Second, and this is the form of witnessing most discussed in historical theory, there is the idea that testimony *is* a vehicle for transmitting a ready-made, authentic understanding or experience. Giving voice to this experience, expressed in the witness's representation of the events, is allegedly a central part of the historian's ethical responsibility.[196] Furthermore, by offering understanding of the events, witnesses become participants in the historian's game of creating historical representations, although testimony has the unique possibility of conveying the authentic experience of what it was like for the witness.

Several influential historical theorists have recently endorsed the idea of testimony as a vehicle of authentic understanding, beyond the objectivist confines of historiography. For example, in a discussion about Primo Levi, Hayden White wrote, "Levi's *Se questo è un uomo* ... derives its power as testimony, less from the scientific and positivistic registration of the 'facts' of Auschwitz, than from its enactment in poetic utterance of *what it felt like* to have had to endure such 'facts.'"[197] Annette Wieviorka appeals to the "extraordinary riches" that testimony brings to historical research as "the encounter with the human voice that traversed history and, in oblique fashion, not factual truth but the more subtle and also indispensable truth of an epoch and of an experience."[198] Similarly, Verónica Tozzi argues that paradigmatic survivor testimony, such as Levi's, is akin to historical research since it addresses specific social questions, such as how collaborationism and the breakdown of the human condition in the death camps were possible. Tozzi contends that both professional historical research and witness accounts offer ways of understanding historical and social processes, and both depend on information chains that rely on relations of trust that are subject to communal checks appropriate for all testimonial reliance.[199] As Spiegel has pointed out, Tozzi's account is at risk of obliterating conceptual

---

[194] Krämer, "Bearing Witness," 32–33.   [195] Felman and Laub, *Testimony.*
[196] See Spiegel, "Future of the Past," 175–177.
[197] White, "Figural Realism in Witness Literature," 123.
[198] Wieviorka, "Witness in History," 396.   [199] Tozzi, "Role of Testimony," 8–9, 15–16.

distinctions between the understanding and knowledge of the past provided by historical research and witness accounts respectively.[200]

That survivor testimony *does* offer ways of understanding life in the death camps is not in doubt. Accounts such as Levi's are indispensable for every attempt to comprehend the dehumanization that was an essential part of the Holocaust.[201] Consequently, Levi's account is an important resource also for historians when they try, like everyone else, to grasp somehow how the events were possible. The crucial concern for historical theory is not, however, the general claim of understanding; rather, it has to do with determining how the understanding provided by witness accounts relates to the presuppositions, a priori concepts and interests of historical research. On this score, however, advocates of testimony have relied on images in which historical research is tantamount to the ideals of the classical Rankean paradigm. Consequently, history is described as antiquarian, objectivist, and in the pursuit of mechanistic contextualization to reveal merely "what happened." Very little is said about history as a specific mode of understanding, which was the core of the evidential paradigm.[202] White was, again, illustrative when he wrote that the historical past is useless since it can only tell us "what people in *other* times, places, and circumstances did in their situation at *that* time and place."[203]

Arguments for the rapprochement between history and testimony rely on the very same opposition that they want to dissolve. Historiography is reduced to ideals of objectivity, universality and reliability, while memory accounts represent the contrary.[204] Arguably, the linguistic turn showed that these classical ideals of historiography were illusory, and, therefore, one may dissolve the opposition by subsuming historiography under the same culturally mediated category as memory. This entire line of reasoning, however, begs one central question: Are the ideals of objectivity, reliability and universality – the founding myths of the Rankean paradigm – the best characterization of the distinctiveness of historical thought? As we have seen, Collingwood and many proponents of the evidential paradigm did not think so. In the following, I show how attending to the specificity of the historical past, produced by the historian's questioning-activity, allows for a deeper understanding of the distinctiveness of historical thought in relation to testimony.

---

[200] Spiegel, "Future of the Past," 172–173.
[201] This claim presupposes, of course, that it is in principle possible to represent so-called limit events in language. For discussion, see Schmidt, "Philosophy of Testimony."
[202] See Jenkins, "Ethical Responsibility," 59–60.   [203] White, *Practical Past*, 9–10.
[204] Klein, "Emergence of *Memory*."

4.7 The Historical Past and Testimonial Understanding

One may exemplify the specificity of the historical past by attending to the ways in which the historian's questioning-activity produces its own object of inquiry. Think of research questions about large-scale social and political processes, such as the causes of the Russian Revolution, the political consequences of the Unification of Germany, or the motivational background of the Holocaust. While facts about a singular event (say, whether there were three days of street-fighting in Brussels in September 1830) may be available via witness accounts, this is not the case for the processes to which the singular event belongs. Large-scale social and political processes, such as the Unification of Germany or the Holocaust, are notional totalities that no one could have possibly witnessed directly. This impossibility is logical, not psychological. Descriptions of historical events by historians employ concepts denoting events that are irreducible to one single happening but stretch out in time and space beyond the reach of the perception of any single human being. A person may witness the looting of a palace or the execution of prisoners at a death camp, but this is not to witness "the Russian Revolution" or "the Holocaust" in the historian's sense of these terms. Furthermore, as narrativist philosophers emphasize, historians may understand historical events in terms of retrospectively constructed analytical concepts and narrative sentences that were not logically available to contemporary witnesses.[205]

One must be careful not to overestimate the force of these considerations in relation to testimony. Advocates of testimony could argue, and correctly so, that historiography is not solely concerned with narrating large-scale processes and retrospectivity. Obviously, historians may be specifically interested in individual accounts of what it was like to live through large-scale historical processes – and an understanding of this subjective side of experience is precisely what testimony may transmit. This is true, but problems arise with the assumption that "understanding" is an item that can be transmitted between historical agents and historians. As we saw in previous sections, there are good arguments to be made for the idea that knowledge about facts is something that can be transmitted. If you tell me that the train leaves at five o'clock, then this knowledge, or at least the justification for the claim in question, is transmitted to me when I take your word for it.[206] It is, however, a completely different thing to say that testimony may transmit understanding or experience. Typically, by the latter terms, one means something that is irreducibly first personal – that is, a process that everyone must (logically) do for themselves. Witnesses cannot simply give

---

[205] Danto, *Analytical Philosophy of History*, 183. See also, Ankersmit's *Narrative Logic*, 15.
[206] Greco, *Transmission of Knowledge*.

their own understanding to the audience in the same sense as one may exchange goods. This is not to deny the fact that testimony may, of course, *lead* to changes in someone's understanding.[207]

The most coherent alternative is to frame the contribution of testimony as an invitation to shared understanding. In this respect, the idea is that witnesses may express an understanding or experience that induces the audience to enter the witnesses' subjective perspective, and thereby get a glimpse of what it was like from their point of view. Now, the key question here is not whether that is possible but whether entering the subjective perspective of the witness is indeed a point of interest for history. Collingwood's answer is affirmatively negative: "the real essence of historical thought," he wrote, "is that it aims at discovering a past which no one remembers or ever did remember, for the reason that no one ever knew it."[208] As previously discussed, the point here is not simply that historians may often retrospectively constitute a past. At issue is also the fact that historical thinking involves viewing the past not by submerging oneself in one individual perspective but rather by viewing a historical agent's perspective as part of a larger whole.[209]

Historical understanding is about viewing the past not from the perspective of victims or of perpetrators but from a view unavailable to both.[210] This is the view of how these perspectives relate to the situation and, equally, how the perspectives themselves serve as the producers and subjects of the very dimension of meaning inherent in the situation they faced. Importantly, this does not entail that historians may never legitimately use testimony as a *complement* for appreciating the lived experience of historical events. This kind of use of testimony is, of course, ubiquitous in historical research and has been developed to perfection in Holocaust studies by scholars such as Christopher Browning and Saul Friedländer. Using testimony as a complement, however, should not be confused with *substitution*, which would be to claim that the text cited from a witness account *is* historical understanding.

There is a conceptual watershed between history and testimony in relation to experience. In testimony, the experience of the witness is both the origin and endpoint of an account. Experience/understanding is that which is to be transmitted, and the process is completed when the message is received as it was sent. For history, the process is reversed: the experience and understanding of the witness is that which is to be explained, the very starting point of analysis. The historian's task is to view an experience critically as the product of

---

[207] Cf. Malfatti, "Understanding and Testimony."
[208] Collingwood, *Principles of History*, 136.
[209] Cf. Collingwood, *Principles of History*, 223; *Idea of History*, 447.
[210] Cf. LaCapra, *History and Memory*, 41–42.

a particular understanding of the world. Accordingly, entering the space of the much-discussed "subjectivity" and "immediacy" of witness accounts, which testimony may offer, is explicitly *not* what historical thinking is about. Critical historical research does not, as Joan W. Scott wrote in her critique of foundationalist claims for experience, deny the existence of subjects, but critical history is different from the endorsement of specific subject-positions from the fact that "it ... interrogates the processes of their creation."[211] Historical thinking involves, in essence, viewing the past as mediated by the conceptual framework of the agents – a framework that also shapes the experience and understanding that agents may try to convey via testimony. In other words, historical thought rejects the immediacy of experience in favour of focusing on the conceptual mediation and renegotiation of experience.[212]

This philosophical elucidation is crucial for understanding the ways in which historical thinking relates to an individual historical agent's testimony. It is not uncommon to believe that there is a direct conflict between the understanding offered in witness accounts and historical research. Wieviorka provides a good example of how this conflict has been framed:

> Can the historian, when face to face with a living person, act morally as a "memory critic"? ... The historian knows that all life stories are constructions but also that these (re)constructions are the very armature, the vertebral column, of life in the present. Historians finds themselves faced with a problem that is almost impossible to resolve because two moral imperatives come into conflict. Each person has the right to fashion his or her own history, to put together what he or she remembers and what he or she forgets in his or her own way.... Each person has an absolute right to his or her memory, which is nothing other than his or her identity, his or her very being. But this right can come into conflict with an imperative of the historian's profession, the imperative of an obstinate quest for the truth.[213]

Contrary to what I have argued, Wieviorka's dilemma assumes that there is harmony between the historian's and the witness's interest in experience. The witness remembers something in a particular way, expressing an understanding tied to her very identity, which, in turn, gives the audience a view as to "what it was like." This account is, allegedly, in conflict with the historian's "quest for the truth." But what, exactly, is the conflict about? Is it that the witness is not expressing genuinely "what it was like" for her? That seems absurd – that is, unless the historian is also the witness's therapist. Thinking historically about

---

[211] Scott, "Evidence of Experience," 797.
[212] This view of experience is an integral feature of research in cultural and oral history. See for example, Abrams, *Oral History,* 34, 46, 55, 130, 137, 163.
[213] Wieviorka, "Witness in History," 395–396.

the testimony, the historian's main interest would, perhaps, be to investigate and explain the ways in which the character of the account relates to questions about the cultural and social conditions of the witness. However, this interest is not in conflict with appreciating the testimony as an expression of what the events felt like for the witness. The witness's interests to tell what her experience was like and the historian's interest to explain the character of experience inhabit completely different registers, making it difficult to understand what the "moral dilemma" is supposed to be. In fact, Wieviorka's alleged dilemma clearly illustrates problems caused by the rapprochement found in recent historical theory. The erroneous supposition that understanding offered by witnesses is in the same game as history produces (false) dilemmas about who should yield and which understanding to accept.

As we have seen, distinguishing the historical past as a product of the historian's questioning-activity offers a way of articulating the distinctiveness of historical thought beyond objectivism. The historical past is the product of a specific form of understanding premised on conceptually distinct points of interest. Why does this matter? First, it shows that abandoning objectivism – which is perceived as a key consequence of the linguistic turn – makes no difference for the conceptual distinction between history and testimony as different forms of understanding. Second, it provides a bulwark against the conceptual rapprochement between history and memory, as detailed in 4.2–4.3. Even if we agree that both historians and witnesses are subject to the linguistic, political and cultural frames of present preconceptions, then from this it does not follow that the very idea of historical understanding, somehow, approaches testimony and cultural memory. Arguably, no human activity can escape preconceptions of the present, but this predicament will in no way diminish the importance of distinguishing between different modes of relating to the past. On the contrary, abandoning objectivism only highlights the urgency of finding more pertinent conceptual tools for distinguishing testimony and history. In the following, I show how the distinction between historical and practical past matters for discussions about the historian's ethical responsibility.

4.8 The Ethics of Historical and Practical Pasts

For many influential historical theorists, testimony is ethically important as political and moral messages about action for us in the present and the future. Contrary to professional history, representations of the past in testimony and fictive works, White argued, provide accounts in which past and present are fused with the aim of answering the question, "What should I do?"[214] As Tozzi

---
[214] White, *Practical Past*, 76–77.

(developing White's account) wrote, testimonies are valuable "not as a journey to the past but as an action in the present."[215] As such, the systematic collection of testimony in the postwar era was undoubtedly shaped by specific social and political purposes.[216] However, the implicit or explicit claim in the ethical turn of historical theory is not empirical but conceptual. To be "ethical" in historical representation *is* to incorporate testimonial accounts that provide practical pasts for aiding action in the present and the future. On this score, Keith Jenkins has explicitly encouraged historians to "take up the cause of human emancipation" by abandoning "truth" in favour of accounts of the past that are politically useful, which means that "to be 'ethical' ... perhaps signals ... the possible end of a history 'of a certain kind.'"[217] One finds a similar juxtaposition of history as objective versus testimony as a source of the ethical in Assmann's work:

> While memory is indispensable, as a view from the inside, to evaluating the events of the past and to creating an ethical stance, history is needed, as a view from the outside, to scrutinize and verify the remembered events.[218]

The so-called ethical turn in historical theory is a movement away from historical pasts and toward practical pasts, and witness accounts are a popular vehicle for the latter.[219] As a result, ethics in historical research seem to depend on the inclusion of accounts that are explicitly not the products of academic historiography and a relativization of the idea that historical understanding is qualitatively distinct from the understanding offered by witnesses. Becoming ethical apparently requires that historians forfeit their profession. This reduction of ethics to practical uses of the past is crucial for explicating White's often quoted and rather puzzling denial of the ethical responsibility of historians *qua* historians: "I ... deny that historians, in their current 'professional' capacity, possess the resources necessary for rendering 'ethically responsible' judgments on whatever it is we mean by 'history.'"[220] This denial makes perfect sense on the premise that "ethics" is about the production of representations of the past that are practically useful, either as moral or political instruction for the present and the future. As White rightly emphasized, such practical representations are precisely what professional historians are *not* supposed to offer. In other words, historians can become "ethical" only by cutting and pasting accounts from practical pasts in testimony and fiction.

This line of reasoning assumes that the historian's ethical commitments belong to the framework of the ethics of witnessing. The consequences are appositely expressed in Jenkins' description of how historians may "ethically"

---

[215] Tozzi, "Role of Testimony," 3. [216] Dean, *Moral Witness*; Wieviorka, *Era of the Witness*.
[217] Jenkins, "Ethical Responsibility," 60, 43. [218] Assman, "History, Memory," 264.
[219] See Spiegel, "Future of the Past," 174–176. [220] White, "Public Relevance," 335.

relate to the catastrophes of the twentieth century. According to Jenkins, "the *historian's* ethical responsibility" is to refrain from representing the horrors, which can only "drown out the screams of its victims," and instead let the past speak "for itself" – in both the speech and the silences of the victims – in order "to ensure that the Holocaust/Auschwitz forever haunts us."[221] Perhaps unwittingly, Jenkins uses the exact same words that are typically used for describing the ethical responsibility of *victim witnesses*. Survivors of the Holocaust were often assigned the "duty to remember" as a moral obligation.[222] Furthermore, considering the fact that "Nie Wieder – Never Again!" is perhaps the most prominent leitmotif in all Western postwar memory politics, it seems that the historian's ethical responsibility amounts to nothing more than the propagation of cosmopolitan memory culture.[223]

The untenability of this approach becomes apparent when one moves from abstract historical theory towards empirical cases of memory accounts. Doing actual research, the historian will face the question of *whose* testimony to cut and paste for becoming "ethical." By what standards should historians judge whether a memory account does indeed support "emancipation"? The answer cannot simply be that historians should favour testimony from "the victims" – at least not since victimization became a popular method for doing politics. As a result, historical research reduces to politics, and ethics tantamount to the historian's judgment concerning just and unjust testimonies. It would be wrong to assume that this position is peculiar to radical historical theorists such as White or Jenkins. Quite the contrary, the very same logic is present in the framework of narratives and counternarratives, where "history" is often described as the official narrative of hegemony and the nation-state, while memory accounts are styled as progressive counternarratives speaking truth to power. Especially in extremely contentious cases, such as the Israel–Palestine conflict or the history of indigenous peoples, it is commonplace to juxtapose history as the story of people in power against memory accounts as the story of the subjugated.[224] To consider history as always partisan is not problematic. As Collingwood's lecture on impartiality articulated, political partisanship is indeed compatible with high scholarly standards in research. But if history is not to be reduced to ideology confirmation, then those scholarly standards cannot themselves be relative to the same partisanship.[225]

---

[221] Jenkins, "Ethical Responsibility," 54–55. See also Spiegel, "Future of the Past," 175–176.
[222] Wieviorka, "Witness in History," 394. [223] Levy and Sznaider, "Memory Unbound."
[224] Abu-Lughod and Sa'di, "Introduction"; Kennedy, "Stolen Generations Testimony"; Klein, "Emergence of *Memory*."
[225] Cf. Paul, *Historians' Virtues*.

Attending to testimony in relation to ethical concerns about "what to do" in the present and future *is* important.[226] Many labels are already in use for this kind of relation to the past. It is called memory, remembrance, commemoration, testimony – the practical past – all of which are *possibly* important concerns for the general health and stability of democratic societies.[227] But adding "history" to that list invites conceptual confusion. Furthermore, if one disagrees with reducing ethics in history to choosing the most progressive political partisanship, one must ask: What is the ethics of history *qua* history? Any sufficient answer to that question must both, (i) avoid outsourcing ethics to practical pasts, and (ii) acknowledge the distinguishing features of historical thinking that this Element has identified. While the key feature of practical relations to the past via testimony is their (perceived) quality of *immediacy* – as authenticity, experience and expression – the distinct feature of historical relations is to understand past experience as *mediated* by the conceptual framework of the agents, which is further investigated by way of the analytical concepts of the historian. The ethics of history *qua* history is about the ethics of understanding experience as conceptually mediated by both past and present historical agents.

The concept of historical past, as articulated in this Element, entails that there are two distinct but integrally connected ethical aspects of historical relations to the past.[228] First, in our attempts historically to understand experience as conceptually mediated by the perspective of the historical agents, there is a challenge to do justice to what that past perspective was. It belongs to the historian's ethical responsibility to preserve the integrity of the historical past – without equating "the historical past" with the historical agent's own understanding of their situation. Furthermore, the task of explaining others' experiences demands scrutiny of the historian's self-understanding. As the philosopher Peter Winch has emphasized, the task of historical understanding is neither to be seen as a process in which actions and utterances of others are subsumed under our own conditions of intelligibility, nor as a process in which the historian simply adopts the historical agent's understanding. Rather, according to Winch, "seriously to study another way [of looking at things] is necessarily to seek to extend our own – not simply to bring the other way within the already existing boundaries of our own."[229]

---

[226] Cf. Little, *Confronting Evil*.   [227] Cf. Lotem, *Dark Pasts*.

[228] The concern for ethics may, again, lead one to question whether Oakeshott's distinction is tenable. Considering that ethics *is* a practical concern, how can history engage with ethics without at the same time being practical? In relation to this concern, I have argued elsewhere that Oakeshott's distinction must be understood only as an analytical tool and not as an absolute separation between unrelated discourses. For detailed discussion, see my book *Primacy of Method*, 79, 81, 90, 93, 96–97.

[229] Winch, *Ethics and Action*, 33.

The past-related ethical responsibility of historians *is* the demand for self-scrutiny. This is an ethical form of responsibility to the extent that historical agents may be *wronged* if we force the meaning of their words, actions and lives to fit the frames of our own preconceptions. Consequently, historians have the ethical responsibility to track how their own self-understanding enters their explanation of the experience and understanding expressed in testimony. This responsibility is distinctly towards the past, and not the present, since the ethical demand is to do justice to the lived world of historical agents. Dead people are as wronged by lies and projection as living people are. This ethical demand does not depend on the psychology of individual historians – whether they happen to "feel" any such responsibility towards the past or not. Rather, the (logical) possibility of being subject to responsibility towards the past follows from the normative implication of historical description.[230]

There is also a second, present-related aspect of the ethics of history *qua* history. Considering that the contemporary world is dominated by practical relations to the past, the ethical responsibility of the historian is to critically examine the conditions of production of "voices of experience" – especially those that are rallying support for social and political action. History is endowed with the task of *resisting* the immediacy of "historical" experience in the present. The reason is not, of course, that listening to expressions of experience via testimony is unimportant. Rather, the reason is that the overwhelming power of complementary authenticities (via audiovisual testimony and artefacts) may, in fact, as Jones has pointed out, make us less disposed to thinking critically and deeply about the political, social and cultural structures that brought about the situation of violence in the first place – which is exactly what historically understanding the conditions of a certain experience may enable us to appreciate.[231] Furthermore, testimony is constantly at the mercy of manipulative forms of remembrance in which victims end up being heard only as instruments for promoting concerns about one's own distress in the present.[232] Contrary to practical uses of the past, the task of history is *not* to call on ready-made images of the past in order to promote action in the present. On the contrary, the task is to critically examine the conditions in which the ready-made images of the past that populate the public sphere were produced.[233]

The present-related task of history is ethical in the sense that critical examination of "experience" is a prerequisite for every just and reflective relation to conflicting collective pasts. The ethics of history is a form of critical cultural

---

[230] For an elaboration of this claim, see my book *Primacy of Method*, 92.
[231] Jones, "Mediated Immediacy," 148.
[232] Jones, "Mediated Immediacy," 148. See also Saupe and Roche, "Testimonies in Historiography," 83.
[233] Cf. Kansteiner, "Finding Meaning," 190.

self-knowledge in which our understanding of the present is explicated through contrasts with the historical past. By explaining the conceptual mediation of the experience of historical agents, one is inevitably also articulating differences in relation to one's own conceptual horizon.[234] As many historical theorists have argued, cultural memory is always-already part of our present understanding.[235] For this very reason, history is needed as the critical method for bringing to light the contours, conflicts and raptures of contemporary memory cultures. If one is not to blindly accept the established hierarchy of victim witnesses that memory cultures offer (that is, which witnesses should be heard first and last), then any ethically responsible decision about "what to do" presupposes the critical and reflective relation to the past that belongs to historical research. Historical thinking provides a form of understanding that witnesses *qua* witnesses can never give us.

5 Conclusion

This Element explored the relation between history and testimony as a question about what it means to know and understand the past historically. In contrast with the recent rapprochement between memory accounts and history in historical theory, I argued for the importance of attending to conceptually distinct relations to the past in historical thinking compared with memory accounts. The distinctiveness of historical thought was explored in relation to questions about knowledge and facts as well as understanding and meaning. Within the former domain, I showed that historical knowledge includes certain basic forms of testimonial reliance, shared with everyday belief acquisition, but that the research practice of history entails autonomous forms of epistemic justification. Considering understanding and meaning, I argued that the distinction between practical and historical relations elucidates the specificity of historical understanding compared with the kind of understanding offered in testimony. All historians are subject to relations with the past in the plural, but this fact does not diminish the importance of articulating the ideal distinction between the historical and the practical past. Without appreciating this fundamental distinction, there will be no conceptual space for the idea of history as a critical questioning-activity about the past.

The focus has been on the elucidation of conceptually distinct approaches and points of interest in historical research. Witnesses may give access to the past as remembered, but that is explicitly not what the historian is seeking – unless, of course, the research is about how the past was remembered at a particular time

---

[234] For an elaboration of this claim, see my "History as Self-Knowledge," 82–112.
[235] Baquero, "Memory, Narrative."

and place. In that case, however, the historian will be pursuing the kind of historical thinking articulated in this Element. Insofar as testimony aims to transmit unprocessed, authentic experience and understanding based on memory, then witnesses are never quite in the same game as historians for whom experience is that which is to be explained. This conceptual division concerning method holds even if both historians and witnesses are subject to present language and culture. Consequently, appealing to the linguistic turn cannot serve as a valid justification for the inclusion of testimony as a vehicle of "ethical" understanding in historiographical discourse.

I wanted to show that historical thinking is something that one can and should delimit carefully. History is neither our only way to relate to the past nor an appropriate standard for evaluating other relations to the past. This is a central insight to be gained from White's *The Practical Past*. Nevertheless, one must keep in mind that history is today a minority movement compared with the booming industry of memory, commemoration and remembrance. This situation forces one to think less sloppily about the meaning of history and the historian's ethical responsibility – if history is not to be assimilated to extinction in cultural memory. Of course, historians are human beings and, as such, just as imbricated in practical pasts as anyone else. Historians do not escape questions about ethics, politics and responsibility as they are generally posed in public life. Yet, it does not follow from the fact that historians are human beings that their ethical responsibility *qua* historians is to lend themselves to whatever cause of remembrance is presently judged to be politically progressive. As I have argued, what ethics means in history should be understood as a question about the ethical significance of elaborating a historical past.

The author is not under the illusion that everyone shares this Element's core idea of history as a critical questioning-activity. Instead of arguing for that view itself, I have shown what the relation to testimony looks like if one accepts the view of history in question. By and large, that view is a constructivist one.[236] Contrary to what is often assumed, I have shown that constructivism does not bring history any closer to the understanding offered in memory accounts. Importantly, by focusing on the historian's questioning-activity, the rejection of testimony from historiography appears in a new light. If history is a distinct form of understanding, then rejecting testimony need not be based on psychological or epistemic reasons. The problem with memory accounts is not that they are inherently unreliable, limited, subjective, and, therefore, incompatible with the historian's quest for objectivity. Rather, the rejection of testimony is

---

[236] For Collingwood's contested relation to constructivism, see Dray, *History as Re-enactment*, 229–271.

motivated by differences in kind between the understanding of past events that witnesses and historians can have and want to have. As Collingwood wrote about the aims of historical understanding, "the truth of which we are in search was not possessed, ready-made, by the writer whom we are studying."[237] This expresses a distinct idea of why testimony is rejected from history: witnesses do not have the kind of knowledge and understanding that historians are looking for. The questioning-activity is the dominant factor in history, as in all science, and this means the historian's logic of questions and answers determines the role of testimony in historical research.

---

[237] Collingwood, *Idea of History*, 377.

Bibliography

Abrams, Lynn, *Oral History Theory*. London: Routledge, 2010.

Abu-Lughod, Lila and Ahmad H. Sa'di, "Introduction: The Claims of Memory," in Ahmad H. Sa'di and Lila Abu-Lughod (eds.), *Nakba: Palestine, 1948, and the Claims of Memory*. New York: Columbia University Press, 2007, pp. 1–24.

Ahlskog, Jonas, "History as Self-Knowledge: Towards Understanding the Existential and Ethical Dimension of the Historical Past," *História da Historiografia* 12:31 (2019), 82–112.

Ahlskog, Jonas, "Michael Oakeshott and Hayden White on the Practical and the Historical Past," *Rethinking History* 20:3 (2016), 375–394.

Ahlskog, Jonas, "Testimony Stops Where History Begins: Understanding and Ethics in Relation to Historical and Practical Pasts," *History and Theory* 63:4 (2024), 23–42.

Ahlskog, Jonas, "The Crisis of Testimony in Historiography," *Journal of the Philosophy of History* 12:1 (2018), 48–70.

Ahlskog, Jonas, *The Primacy of Method in Historical Research: Philosophy of History and the Perspective of Meaning*. London: Routledge, 2021.

Ahlskog, Jonas and Giuseppina D'Oro, "Imagination and Revision," in Chiel van den Akker (ed.), *The Routledge Companion to Historical Theory*. New York: Routledge, 2022, pp. 215–233.

Ankersmit, Frank, *Narrative Logic: A Semantic Analysis of the Historian's Language*. The Hague: Martinus Nijhoff, 1983.

Ankersmit, Frank, *Sublime Historical Experience*. Stanford: Stanford University Press, 2005.

Barash, Jeffrey Andrew, *Collective Memory and the Historical Past*. Chicago: The University of Chicago Press, 2016.

Assmann, Aleida, "History, Memory, and the Genre of Testimony," *Poetics Today* 27:2 (2006), 261–273.

Assmann, Aleida, "Transformations between History and Memory," *Social Research* 75:1 (2008), 49–72.

Baquero, Rafael Pérez, "Memory, Narrative, and Conflict in Writing the Past: When Historians Undergo Ethical and Political Strains," *História da Historiografia* 13:32 (2020), 47–81. https://doi.org/10.15848/hh.v13i32.1494.

Beiser, Frederick, "Historicism," in Chiel van den Akker (ed.), *The Routledge Companion to Historical Theory*. New York: Routledge, 2022, pp. 3–17.

Bentley, Michael, "The Turn towards 'Science': Historians Delivering Untheorized Truth," in Nancy Partner and Sarah Foot (eds.), *The Sage Handbook of Historical Theory*. London: Sage, 2013, pp. 10–22.

Berger, Stefan and Chris Lorenz (eds.), *Nationalizing the Past: Historians as Nation Builders in Modern Europe*. London: Palgrave Mcmillan, 2010.

Bevernage, Berber, *History, Memory, and State-Sponsored Violence*. New York: Routledge, 2012.

Bevernage, Berber, "Time, Presence, and Historical Injustice," *History and Theory* 47:2 (2008), 149–167.

Bloch, Marc, "Reflections of an Historian on the False News of the War" [1921], tran. James P. Holoka, *Michigan War Studies Review* 51 (2013), 1–12. www.miwsr.com/2013/downloads/2013-051.pdf.

Bloch, Marc, *The Historian's Craft*, trans. Peter Putnam. Manchester: Manchester University Press, 1954.

Bourke, Joanna, "Introduction: 'Remembering' War," *Journal of Contemporary History* 39:4 (2004), 473–485.

Browning, Christopher R., *Remembering Survival: Inside a Nazi Slave-Labor Camp*. New York: Norton, 2010.

Burke, Peter, "History as Social Memory," in his *Varieties of Cultural History*. Cambridge: Polity Press, 1997, pp. 43–59.

Cath, Yuri, *Knowing What It Is Like*. Cambridge: Cambridge University Press, 2024.

Coady, Cecil Anthony John, *Testimony: A Philosophical Study*. Oxford: Clarendon Press, 1992.

Collingwood, Robin George, *The Idea of History*, ed. Jan van der Dussen. Oxford: Oxford University Press, 1993.

Collingwood, Robin George, "The Limits of Historical Knowledge," in William Debbins (ed.), *Essays in the Philosophy of History*. Austin: University of Texas Press, 1965, pp. 90–103.

Collingwood, Robin George, *The Principles of History and Other Writings in the Philosophy of History*, ed. William Herbert Dray and Jan van der Dusen. Oxford: Oxford University Press, 1999.

Confino, Alon, "History and Memory," in Axel Schneider and Daniel Woolf (eds.), *The Oxford History of Historical Writing*, vol. 5, *Historical Writing since 1945*. Oxford: Oxford University Press, 2011, pp. 46–51. Online https://doi.org/10.1093/oso/9780199225996.003.0003.

Cubitt, Geoffrey, "History of Memory," in Marek Tamm and Peter Burke (eds.), *Debating New Approaches to History*. London: Bloomsbury Academic, 2019, pp. 127–158.

D'Amico, Robert, "Historicism," in Aviezer Tucker (ed.), *A Companion to the Philosophy of History and Historiography*. Chichester: Wiley-Blackwell, 2011, pp. 243–253.

Danto, Arthur, *Analytical Philosophy of History*. Cambridge: Cambridge University Press, 1965.

Day, Mark, "Our Relations with the Past," *Philosophia* 36 (2008), 417–427.

Day, Mark, *The Philosophy of History: An Introduction*. London: Continuum, 2008.

De Certeau, Michel, *Heterologies: Discourse on the Other*, trans. Brian Massumi. Minneapolis: University of Minnesota Press, 1986.

Dean, Carolyn J., *The Moral Witness: Trials and Testimony after Genocide*. Cornell: Cornell University Press, 2019.

Dray, William Herbert, *History as Re-enactment: R. G. Collingwood's Idea of History*. Oxford: Clarendon Press, 1995.

Dray, William Herbert, *Philosophy of History*. Englewood Cliffs: Prentice-Hall, 1964.

Droysen, Johann Gustav, *Historik: Vorlesungen über Enzyklopädie und Methodologie der Geschichte*. Munich: Oldenbourg, 1937.

Eskildsen, Kasper Rijsberg, "Inventing the Archive: Testimony and Virtue in Modern Historiography," *History of the Human Sciences* 26:4 (2013), 8–26.

Eskildsen, Kasper Rijsberg, "Leopold Ranke's Archival Turn: Location and Evidence in Modern Historiography," *Modern Intellectual History* 5:3 (2008), 425–453.

Eskildsen, Kasper Rijsberg, "Relics of the Past: Antiquarianism and Archival Authority in Enlightenment Germany," *Storia della Storiografia* 68:2 (2016), 69–84. https://doi.org/10.1400/240639.

Faulkner, Paul, "On Telling and Trusting." *Mind* 116:464 (2007), 875–902.

Faulkner, Paul, *Knowledge on Trust*. Oxford: Oxford University Press, 2011.

Felman, Shoshana and Dori Laub, *Testimony: Crises of Witnessing in Literature, Psychoanalysis, and History*. New York: Routledge, 1992.

Forcinito, Ana, "*Testimonio*: The Witness, the Truth, and the Inaudible," in Y. Martínez-San Miguel, Yolanda Ben Sifuentes-Jáuregui and Marisa Belausteguigoitia (eds.), *Critical Terms in Caribbean and Latin American Thought: New Directions in Latino American Cultures*. New York: Palgrave Macmillan, 2016, pp. 239–251. Online https://doi.org/10.1057/9781137 547903_22.

Foucault, Michel, *Archaeology of Knowledge*, trans. Alan Mark Sheridan Smith. New York: Routledge, 2002.

Foucault, Michel, "Nietzsche, Genealogy, History," in Paul Rabinow (ed.), *The Foucault Reader*. New York: Pantheon Books, 1984, pp. 76–101.

Fricker, Miranda, *Epistemic Injustice: Power and the Ethics of Knowing*. Oxford: Oxford University Press, 2007.

Frum, David, "The New History Wars: Inside the Strife Set Off by an Essay from the President of the American Historical Association," *The Atlantic*, October 20, 2022. www.theatlantic.com/ideas/archive/2022/10/american-his torical-association-james-sweet/671853/.

Gadamer, Hans-Georg, *Truth and Method*, trans. Joel Weinsheimer and Donald G. Marshall, 2nd ed. New York: Continuum, 2004.

Gelfert, Axel, *A Critical Introduction to Testimony*. London: Bloomsbury Academic, 2014.

Gelfert, Axel, "Testimony," in *Routledge Encyclopedia of Philosophy*. Taylor and Francis, 2018. https://doi.org/10.4324/0123456789-P049-2. www.rep.routledge.com/articles/thematic/testimony/v-2.

Gil, Thomas, "Leopold Ranke," in Aviezer Tucker (ed.), *A Companion to the Philosophy of History and Historiography*. Chichester: Wiley-Blackwell, 2011, pp. 383–393.

Ginzburg, Carlo, "Clues: Roots of an Evidential Paradigm," in *Clues, Myths and the Historical Method*, trans. John Tedeschi and Anne C. Tedeschi. Baltimore: Johns Hopkins University Press, 1986, pp. 87–113.

Ginzburg, Carlo, "Just One Witness," in Saul Friedlander (ed.), *Probing the Limits of Representation: Nazism and the "Final Solution."* Cambridge, MA: Harvard University Press, 1992, pp. 82–96.

Goldstein, Leon, *The What and the Why of History: Philosophical Essays*. Leiden: Brill, 1996.

Grafton, Anthony, *The Footnote: A Curious History*. Cambridge, MA: Harvard University Press, 1999.

Greco, John, *The Transmission of Knowledge*. Cambridge: Cambridge University Press, 2020.

Hardwig, John, "The Role of Trust in Knowledge," *The Journal of Philosophy* 88:12 (1991), 693–708. https://doi.org/10.2307/2027007.

Hinchman, Edward S., "Assurance and Warrant," *Philosopher's Imprint* 14 (2014), 1–58.

Hinchman, Edward S., "Telling as Inviting to Trust," *Philosophy and Phenomenological Research* 70:3 (2005), 562–587.

Hudson, Nicholas, *Writing and European Thought, 1600–1830*. Cambridge: Cambridge University Press, 1994.

Huizinga, Johan, *The Autumn of the Middle Ages*, trans. Rodney J. Payton and Ulrich Mammitzsch. Chicago: University of Chicago Press, 1996.

Hutton, Patrick H., *History as an Art of Memory*. Hanover: University Press of New England, 1993.

Iggers, G. G., "Historicism," in Philip Paul Wiener (ed.), *The Dictionary of the History of Ideas*, vol. 2. New York: Scribner, 1974, 456–463.

Jardine, Nick, "Explanatory Genealogies and Historical Testimony," *Episteme* 5:2 (2008), 160–179.

Jenkins, Keith, "Ethical Responsibility and the Historian: On the Possible End of a History 'of a Certain Kind'," *History and Theory* 43:4 (2004), 43–60.

Jones, Sara, "Mediated Immediacy: Constructing Authentic Testimony in Audio-Visual Media," *Rethinking History* 21:2 (2017), 135–153.

Jones, Sara, "Testimony through Culture: Towards a Theoretical Framework," *Rethinking History* 23:3 (2019), 257–278.

Jones, Sara and Roger Woods, "Introduction: Testimony in Culture and Cultures of Testimony," in Sarah Jones and Roger Woods (eds.), *The Palgrave Handbook of Testimony and Culture*. Cham: Palgrave MacMillan, 2023, pp. 1–20. https://doi.org/10.1007/978-3-031-13794-5_1.

Kansteiner, Wulf, "Finding Meaning in Memory: A Methodological Critique of Collective Memory Studies," *History and Theory* 41:2 (2002), 179–197.

Kant, Immanuel, "On a Supposed Right to Tell Lies from Benevolent Motives," trans. Thomas Kingsmill Abbott, in *Critique of Practical Reason and Other Works on the Theory of Ethics*, 4th revised ed., London: Longmans, Green, 1889, pp. 361–365.

Kennedy, Rick, *A History of Reasonableness: Testimony and Authority in the Art of Thinking*. Rochester: The University of Rochester Press, 2004.

Kennedy, Roseanne, "Stolen Generations Testimony: Trauma, Historiography, and the Question of Truth," in Robert Perks and Alistair Thomson (eds.), *The Oral History Reader*, second ed. London: Routledge, 2006, pp. 506–521.

Kilby, Jane and Antony Rowland (eds.), *The Future of Testimony: Interdisciplinary Perspectives on Witnessing*. New York: Routledge, 2014.

Klein, Kerwin Lee, "On the Emergence of *Memory* in Historical Discourse," *Representations* 69 (2000), 127–150.

Kleinberg, Ethan, *Haunting History: For a Deconstructive Approach to the Past*. Stanford: Stanford University Press, 2017.

Kosso, Peter, "Historical Evidence and Epistemic Justification: Thucydides as a Case Study," *History and Theory* 32:1 (1993), 1–13.

Krämer, Sibylle and Sigrid Weigel, "Converging the Yet-Separate Theoretical Discourses of Testimony Studies," in Sybille Krämer and Sigrid Weigel (eds.), *Testimony/Bearing Witness: Epistemology, Ethics, History and Culture*. London: Rowman & Littlefield, 2017, pp. ix–xli.

Krämer, Sybille, "Bearing Witness as Truth Practice: The Twofold – Discursive and Existential – Character of Telling Truth in Testimony," in Sarah Jones and Roger Woods (eds.), *The Palgrave Handbook of Testimony and Culture*.

Cham: Palgrave MacMillan, 2023, pp. 23–39. Online https://doi.org/10.1007/978-3-031-13794-5_2.

Kuukkanen, Jouni-Matti, *Postnarrativist Philosophy of Historiography*. Hampshire: Palgrave Macmillan, 2015.

LaCapra, Dominick, *History and Memory after Auschwitz*. Ithaca: Cornell University Press, 1998.

Lackey, Jennifer, *Learning from Words: Testimony as a Source of Knowledge*. Oxford: Oxford University Press, 2008.

Leonard, Nick, "Epistemological Problems of Testimony," in Edward N. Zalta and Uri Nodelman (eds.), *The Stanford Encyclopedia of Philosophy*, Spring 2023 ed. https://plato.stanford.edu/archives/spr2023/entries/testimony-episprob/.

Levy, Daniel and Natan Sznaider, "Memory Unbound: The Holocaust and the Formation of Cosmopolitan Memory," *European Journal of Social Theory* 5:1 (2002), 87–106.

Little, Daniel, *Confronting Evil in History*. Cambridge: Cambridge University Press, 2022.

Lorenz, Chris, "Historical Knowledge and Historical Reality: A Plea for 'Internal Realism'," *History and Theory* 33:3 (1994), 297–327.

Lorenz, Chris, "It Takes Three to Tango: History between the 'Practical' and the 'Historical' Past," *Storia della Storiografia* 65:1 (2014), 29–46.

Lorenz, Chris, "Scientific Historiography," in Aviezer Tucker (ed.), *A Companion to the Philosophy of History and Historiography*. Chichester: Wiley-Blackwell, 2011, pp. 393–404.

Lorenz, Chris and Berber Bevernage (eds.), *Breaking Up Time: Renegotiating the Borders between Present, Past and Future*. Göttingen: Vandenhoeck & Ruprecht, 2013.

Lotem, Itay, *Dealing with Dark Pasts: A European History of Auto-Critical Memory in Global Perspective*. Cambridge: Cambridge University Press, 2025.

Malfatti, Federica Isabella, "On Understanding and Testimony," *Erkenntnis* 86 (2021), 1345–1365.

Margalit, Avishai, *The Ethics of Memory*. Cambridge, MA: Harvard University Press, 2004.

McMyler, Benjamin, *Testimony, Trust and Authority*. New York: Oxford University Press, 2011.

Megill, Allan, "History, Memory, Identity," *History of the Human Sciences* 11:3 (1998), 37–62.

Moran, Richard, "Getting Told and Being Believed," *Philosophers' Imprint* 5:5 (2005), 1–29.

Mudrovcic, María Inés, *Conceptualizing the History of the Present Time*. Cambridge: Cambridge University Press, 2024.

Mudrovcic, María Inés, "Time, History, and Philosophy of History," *Journal of the Philosophy of History* 8 (2014), 1–26.

Murphey, Murray Griffin, *Truth and History*. New York: State University of New York Press, 2009.

Nora, Pierre, "Between Memory and History: *Les Lieux de Mémoire*," *Representations* 26 (1989), 7–24.

Nora, Pierre, "The Era of Commemoration," in Pierre Nora and Lawrence D. Kritzman (eds.), *Realms of Memory: The Construction of the French Past*, vol. 3, trans. Arthur Goldhammer. New York: Columbia University Press, 1998, pp. 609–637.

Oakeshott, Michael, *Experience and Its Modes*. Cambridge: Cambridge University Press, 1933.

Oakeshott, Michael, *On History and Other Essays*. Oxford: Basil Blackwell, 1983.

Oakeshott, Michael, *Rationalism in Politics and Other Essays*. Indianapolis: Liberty Fund, 1991.

Ohara, João, *The Theory and Philosophy of History: Global Variations*. Cambridge: Cambridge University Press, 2022.

Oreskes, Naomi, *Why Trust Science?* Princeton: Princeton University Press, 2021.

O'Sullivan, Luke, *Oakeshott on History*. Exeter: Imprint Academic, 2003.

Paul, Herman, *Historians' Virtues: From Antiquity to the Twenty-First Century*. Cambridge: Cambridge University Press, 2022.

Paul, Herman, *Key Issues in Historical Theory*. London: Routledge, 2015.

Pollock, Joey, "Testimonial Knowledge and Content Preservation," *Philosophical Studies* 180 (2023), 3073–3097.

Ricoeur, Paul, *Memory, History, Forgetting*, trans. Kathleen Blamey and David Pellauer. Chicago: The University of Chicago Press, 2004.

Runia, Eelco, *Moved by the Past: Discontinuity and Historical Mutation*. New York: Columbia University Press, 2014.

Sabrow, Martin, "Der Zeitzeuge als Wanderer zwischen zwei Welten," in Martin Sabrow and Norbert Frei (eds.), *Die Geburt des Zeitzeugen nach 1945*. Göttingen: Wallstein, 2012, pp. 13–33.

Saupe, Achim and Helen Roche, "Testimonies in Historiography and Oral History," in Sarah Jones and Roger Woods (eds.), *The Palgrave Handbook of Testimony and Culture*. Cham: Palgrave MacMillan, 2023, pp. 65–91. Online https://doi.org/10.1007/978-3-031-13794-5_4.

Schmidt, Sibylle, "The Philosophy of Testimony: Between Epistemology and Ethics," in Sybille Krämer and Sigrid Weigel (eds.), *Testimony/Bearing Witness: Epistemology, Ethics, History and Culture*. London: Rowman & Littlefield, 2017, pp. 259–275.

Scott, Joan W., "The Evidence of Experience," *Critical Inquiry* 17:4 (1991), 773–797.

Spiegel, Gabrielle M., "The Future of the Past: History, Memory and the Ethical Imperatives of Writing History," *Journal of the Philosophy of History* 8:2 (2014), 149–179.

Stone, Dan, "History, Memory, Testimony," in Jane Kilby and Antony Rowland (eds.), *The Future of Testimony: Interdisciplinary Perspectives on Witnessing*. New York: Routledge, 2014, pp. 17–30.

Tamm, Marek, "Beyond History and Memory: New Perspectives in Memory Studies," *History Compass* 11:6 (2013), 458–473.

Tamm, Marek, "Memory," in Chiel van den Akker (ed.), *The Routledge Companion to Historical Theory*. New York: Routledge, 2022, pp. 544–558.

Tamm, Marek, "Truth, Objectivity and Evidence in History Writing," *Journal of the Philosophy of History* 8:2 (2014), 265–290.

Thompson, Martyn, *Michael Oakeshott and the Cambridge School on the History of Political Thought*. London: Routledge, 2019.

Thucydides, *The Peloponnesian War*, trans. Steven Lattimore. Indianapolis: Hackett, 1998.

Tosh, John, *The Pursuit of History: Aims, Methods and New Directions in the Study of Modern History*. Harlow: Pearson, 2010.

Tozzi, Verónica, "The Epistemic and Moral Role of Testimony," *History and Theory* 51:1 (2012), 1–17.

Tucker, Aviezer, *Historiographic Reasoning*. Cambridge: Cambridge University Press, 2025.

Tucker, Aviezer, *Our Knowledge of the Past: A Philosophy of Historiography*. Cambridge: Cambridge University Press, 2004.

Van der Dussen, Jan, *History as a Science: The Philosophy of R. G. Collingwood*. The Hague: Martinus Nijhoff, 1981.

Van der Dussen, Jan, "The Case for Imagination: Defending the Human Factor and Narrative," in Nancy Partner and Sarah Foot (eds.), *The Sage Handbook of Historical Theory*. London: Sage, 2013, pp. 41–67.

Van der Heiden, Gert-Jan, *The Voice of Misery: A Continental Philosophy of Testimony*. New York: SUNY Press, 2020.

White, Hayden, "Figural Realism in Witness Literature," *Parallax* 10:1 (2004), 113–124.

White, Hayden, *The Practical Past*. Evanston: Northwestern University Press, 2014.

White, Hayden, "The Public Relevance of Historical Studies: A Reply to Dirk Moses," *History and Theory* 44:3 (2005), 333–338.

Wieviorka, Annette, *The Era of the Witness*, trans. Jared Stark. Ithaca: Cornell University Press, 2006.

Wieviorka, Annette, "The Witness in History," *Poetics Today* 27:2 (2006), 385–397.

Williams, Bernard, "Deciding to Believe," in his *Problems of the Self*. Cambridge: Cambridge University Press, 1973, pp. 136–151.

Wilson, Richard Ashby, *Writing History in International Criminal Trials*. Cambridge: Cambridge University Press, 2011.

Winch, Peter, *Ethics and Action*. London: Routledge, 1972.

Winter, Jay, "The Generation of Memory: Reflections on the 'Memory Boom' in Contemporary Historical Studies," *Canadian Military History* 10:3 (2001), 57–66.

Wittgenstein, Ludwig, *Culture and Value*, trans. Peter Winch. Oxford: Basil Blackwell, 1970.

Woolf, Daniel, *A Concise History of History: Global Historiography from Antiquity to the Present*. Cambridge: Cambridge University Press, 2019.

Woolf, Daniel, *The Social Circulation of the Past: English Historical Culture 1500–1730*. Oxford: Oxford University Press, 2003.

Cambridge Elements

Historical Theory and Practice

Daniel Woolf
Queen's University, Ontario

Daniel Woolf is Professor of History at Queen's University, where he served for ten years as Principal and Vice-Chancellor, and has held academic appointments at a number of Canadian universities. He is the author or editor of several books and articles on the history of historical thought and writing, and on early modern British intellectual history, including most recently *A Concise History of History* (CUP 2019). He is a Fellow of the Royal Historical Society, the Royal Society of Canada, and the Society of Antiquaries of London. He is married with three adult children.

Editorial Board
Dipesh Chakrabarty, *University of Chicago*
Marnie Hughes-Warrington, *University of South Australia*
Ludmilla Jordanova, *University of Durham*
Angela McCarthy, *University of Otago*
María Inés Mudrovcic, *Universidad Nacional de Comahue*
Herman Paul, *Leiden University*
Stefan Tanaka, *University of California, San Diego*
Richard Ashby Wilson, *University of Connecticut*

About the Series
Cambridge Elements in Historical Theory and Practice is a series intended for a wide range of students, scholars, and others whose interests involve engagement with the past. Topics include the theoretical, ethical, and philosophical issues involved in doing history, the interconnections between history and other disciplines and questions of method, and the application of historical knowledge to contemporary global and social issues such as climate change, reconciliation and justice, heritage, and identity politics.

Cambridge Elements

Historical Theory and Practice

Elements in the Series

Writing the History of Global Slavery
Trevor Burnard

Plural Pasts: Historiography between Events and Structures
Arthur Alfaix Assis

The History of Knowledge
Johan Östling and David Larsson Heidenblad

Conceptualizing the History of the Present Time
María Inés Mudrovcic

Writing the History of the African Diaspora
Toyin Falola

Dealing with Dark Pasts: A European History of Auto-Critical Memory in Global Perspective
Itay Lotem

A Human Rights View of the Past
Antoon De Baets

Historians' Autobiographies as Historiographical Inquiry: A Global Perspective
Jaume Aurell

Historiographic Reasoning
Aviezer Tucker

Pragmatism and Historical Representation
Serge Grigoriev

History And Hermeneutics
Paul Fairfield

Testimony and Historical Knowledge: Authority, Evidence and Ethics in Historiography
Jonas Ahlskog

A full series listing is available at: www.cambridge.org/EHTP

For EU product safety concerns, contact us at Calle de José Abascal, 56–1°, 28003 Madrid, Spain or eugpsr@cambridge.org.

www.ingramcontent.com/pod-product-compliance
Lightning Source LLC
LaVergne TN
LVHW011856060526
838200LV00054B/4371